P9-DFS-610

One-Dish Vegetarian Meals

ALSO BY ROBIN ROBERTSON

Quick Fix Vegetarian

Peanut Butter Planet

Carb-Conscious Vegetarian

Fresh from the Vegetarian Slow Cooker

Vegan Planet

The Vegetarian Meat & Potatoes Cookbook

Pasta for All Seasons

Rice & Spice

The Sacred Kitchen (with Jon Robertson)

The Vegetarian Chili Cookbook

Some Like It Hot

The Soy Gourmet

366 Simply Delicious Dairy-Free Recipes

366 Healthful Ways to Cook Tofu and Other Meat Alternatives

One-Dish

VEGETARIAN

Meals

150 Easy,
Wholesome,
and Delicious
Soups, Stews,
Casseroles,
Stir-Fries,
Pastas, Rice
Dishes, Chilis,
and More

ROBIN ROBERTSON

THE HARVARD COMMON PRESS · BOSTON, MASSACHUSETTS

The Harvard Common Press
535 Albany Street
Boston, Massachusetts 02118
www.harvardcommonpress.com

Copyright © 2007 by Robin Robertson
Cover photography copyright © 2007 by Eskite Photography

All rights reserved. No part of this publication may be reproduced or
transmitted in any form or by any means, electronic or mechanical,
including photocopying, recording, or any information storage or retrieval
system, without permission in writing from the publisher.

Printed in the United States of America
Printed on acid-free paper

Library of Congress Cataloging-in-Publication Data

Robertson, Robin (Robin G.)
  One-dish vegetarian meals : 150 easy, wholesome, and delicious soups,
stews, casseroles, stir-fries, pastas, rice dishes, chilis, and more / Robin
Robertson.
      p. cm.
   Includes index.
    ISBN 978-1-55832-369-8 (hardcover : alk. paper) —
ISBN 978-1-55832-370-4 (pbk. : alk. paper)
   1. Vegetarian cookery. 2. One-dish meals. I. Title.
   TX837.R62496 2007
   641.5'636—dc22
                                                    2007002513

Special bulk-order discounts are available on this and other Harvard
Common Press books. Companies and organizations may purchase books
for premiums or resale, or may arrange a custom edition, by contacting
the Marketing Director at the address above.

Cover recipe: Vegetable Tagine, page 144
Back cover recipe: Bell Peppers Stuffed with Rice, Spinach, and Sun-Dried
Tomatoes, page 67

Interior design by Richard Oriolo
Cover design by Night & Day Design
Cover photography by Eskite Photography
Food styling by Andrea Lucich
Prop styling by Carol Hacker

10 9 8 7 6 5 4 3 2 1

CONTENTS

INTRODUCTION

Certain recipes we return to again and again, particularly those satisfying one-dish family favorites that make us feel good all over. These are the recipes that are so flavorful, they taste like you've spent all day in the kitchen. That's what *One-Dish Vegetarian Meals* is about—a comprehensive new collection of vegetarian favorites filled with nourishing and delicious one-dish recipes for every season and every reason.

The recipes in this book complement our busy lifestyles and our desire to eat healthful and great-tasting food without a lot of fuss. These full-flavored vegetarian dishes are economical, simple to prepare, and a pleasure to eat. The versatile recipes work equally well for simple weeknight dinners or for casual entertaining. Many of the dishes can be made ahead and popped in the oven to heat just before mealtime. They also lend themselves to easy transporting, making them ideal for potluck gatherings. Many are great for feeding a crowd.

One-Dish Vegetarian Meals is filled with great-tasting choices for hearty comfort-food meals, including satisfying soups, stews, and chilis; lightning-quick stir-fries and sautés; comforting casseroles, lasagne, and baked stuffed vegetables; and pages of tempting pasta dishes and main-dish salads. It provides you with more than 150 of the best one-dish recipes specially chosen from three of my classic cookbooks, *Rice & Spice, Pasta for All Seasons*, and *The Vegetarian Chili Cookbook*, together for the first time in one easy-to-use volume.

The globally inspired recipes offer tremendous variety and sophisticated flavors that will please vegetarians and non-vegetarians alike with choices such as Lentil Soup with Chard and Orzo; Autumn Harvest Lasagne; Baked Polenta with Red Beans and Fresh Tomato Salsa; Rigatoni with Radicchio, Italian Peppers, and Leeks; Orange-Glazed Tofu Strips over Rice; Pumpkin and Black Bean Chili; and many more.

Many of these recipes have long been personal favorites of my family and friends. It is my hope that they will soon become your favorites as well.

A VEGETARIAN

KITCHEN

Before digging into the recipes, I'd like to give you some insights about some of the ingredients you'll be using to create them. I also want to share my professional cooking tips that can help you prepare delicious and satisfying meals with ease and confidence.

Because it is important to include a wide variety of beans, grains, vegetables, and other plant-based ingredients in a vegetarian diet, I have made a special effort to do so in these recipes—not just for the obvious nutritional value, but also to add interest and variety to your meals.

About Rice

Rice is an important and versatile ingredient in any vegetarian kitchen. It is nutritious, easy to digest, contains no cholesterol or saturated fat, and is rich in vitamins and minerals, making it a natural choice for healthy eating. Since many varieties of rice cook in 20 minutes or less, a meal made with fresh-cooked rice can be ready in less than half an hour.

COOKING RICE

Whether it's seasoned with toasted sesame oil, tamari, or grated ginger, or enlivened with lemon zest or fresh herbs, rice easily adapts to most any ethnic flavor nuance that comes its way.

A simple trick to transform any rice into a welcome convenience food is to cook a quantity in advance for later use. Rice can be easily reheated without compromising its taste or texture. In addition, rice can be kept warm for up to 30 minutes after cooking and still retain its character.

RICE COOKING CHART

The following chart shows cooking times and water amounts for the most common types of rice. To cook, combine the rice and water in a saucepan. Cover and bring to a boil. Reduce the heat to low, add salt to the water, and simmer, covered, until the water is absorbed. Soaking, altitude, and the age of the grain may all influence the outcome, so be sure to monitor and test for doneness. On the average, 2 cups of raw rice will yield approximately 6 cups of cooked rice. In each case, remove the pot from the heat at end of the cooking time and allow the rice to rest, covered for 5 minutes. For mixed rice blends, parboiled rice, and instant rice, follow the cooking directions on the package.

RICE (2 CUPS)	WATER	COOKING TIME
Basmati rice	3¾–4 cups	18–20 minutes
Black rice	4 cups	30 minutes
Jasmine rice	3½ cups	15 minutes
Long-grain brown rice	4 cups	30 minutes
Long-grain white rice	4 cups	18–20 minutes
Red rice	4¼ cups	35–40 minutes
Short-grain brown rice	5 cups	45–50 minutes
Sweet or sticky rice	3 cups	15–20 minutes
Wild rice	5 cups	40–50 minutes

About Other Grains

While rice is the most frequently used grain in these recipes, several other wholesome grains can provide great taste as well as economical sources of high-quality nutrition. For variety, try substituting other grains for the rice in some of these recipes. Among the many grains to choose from are millet, quinoa, barley, wheat, kamut, and many others. These grains can be used in soups, stuffings, pilafs, puddings, and desserts, as well as to make breads and pastas. Each type of grain has its own nutritional value, unique flavor, and cooking characteristics. When combined with beans, vegetables, and seasonings, grains provide great taste and texture, in addition to good nutrition. Get familiar with them and you'll significantly expand your recipe repertoire.

STORING AND COOKING OTHER GRAINS

Most whole raw grains can be stored unrefrigerated in tightly covered containers, as long as they are kept away from heat, light, and humidity. To prolong their shelf life, you can store uncooked grains in the refrigerator or freezer.

Grains should be rinsed before using to remove loose hulls, dust, and other impurities.

To intensify the flavor of a grain, you may toast it lightly in a dry skillet before cooking. Most grains can be cooked in a pot with about two times as much water as grain, or more, depending on the cooking time. Bring the water to a boil, cover, reduce the heat to low, and simmer until tender, adding more water along the way if necessary. The water will be absorbed into the grain.

One cup of uncooked grain will yield an average of 3 cups of cooked grain. Longer-cooking grains benefit from cooking in a pressure cooker, while grains with shorter cooking times taste great prepared pilaf style, which begins with sautéing the grains in oil and then adding liquid to finish the cooking.

GRAIN COOKING CHART

Following is a chart of average cooking times for several grains using the stove-top cooking method. Be sure to salt the water once it comes to a boil. Let the grains stand, covered, for 5 minutes after cooking, then fluff with a fork before serving.

GRAIN (1 CUP)	WATER	COOKING TIME
Barley	3 cups	1 hour
Buckwheat (kasha)	2½ cups	20 minutes
Bulgur	2 cups	15 minutes
Couscous	1½ cups	10 minutes
Millet	2 cups	30 minutes
Quinoa	2 cups	20 minutes
Spelt	3½ cups	1 hour

About Pasta

Pasta comes in all sizes, from the tiny acini di pepe (peppercorn-shaped pasta used in soups) to the conchiglie (large shells) used for stuffing. Pastas have so many varieties that they are given poetic names that describe their shapes, such as mostaccioli (little mustaches) and farfalle (butterflies). Strand pastas include the delicate capelli d'angelo or angel hair, and the ubiquitous spaghetti, linguine, and fettuccine.

Most traditional Italian pasta is made from enriched semolina flour ground from hard durum wheat. For those who are wheat sensitive, natural foods stores carry pastas made from quinoa, corn, spelt, and rice. Pasta can also vary in color and taste. A variety of herbs, vegetables, and seasonings can be added to pasta dough to produce artichoke, tomato, and spinach pastas, or more exotic varieties flavored with ingredients such as wild mushrooms, beets, and chiles. Dried pasta is the most common and inexpensive type and offers the most variety of shapes. Fresh pasta is more costly and usually available commercially only in strands or sheets. Several high-quality brands of both dried and fresh pasta can easily be found in well-stocked supermarkets and specialty food shops.

COOKING PASTA

Dried pasta takes longer to cook than fresh, usually 3 to 15 minutes, depending on the shape and quality of the pasta. The preferred cooked texture is slightly firm, called *al dente* or "to the teeth." Fresh pasta cooks in 1 to 3 minutes, producing more tender results.

The basic cooking method is to cook pasta in a large amount of rapidly boiling salted water (a minimum of 5 quarts per pound) until done. To save time, be sure to add the salt after the water comes to a boil, since unsalted water boils faster. Also keep a lid on your pot when bringing the water to a boil. Once the pasta is added to the pot, cook uncovered, stirring frequently.

Test for doneness by retrieving a piece of pasta from the water and biting into it. Since it is important not to overcook pasta, it is best not to rely solely on the cooking time recommended on the box, but to begin testing a few minutes beforehand to ensure that it is done to your liking. For a pasta that is supposed to be cooked in 10 minutes, for example, start testing it for doneness after about 8 minutes. Pasta cooking times are measured beginning from when the water returns to a boil after the pasta has been added.

Be sure to stir the pasta several times during the cooking process to prevent pieces from sticking to the bottom of the pot and each other. Drain pasta thoroughly in a colander before adding sauces or other ingredients.

Cooked pasta should only be rinsed after draining when one is using it in pasta salads or other cold dishes, or if it will not be used immediately. In such an instance, rinse the pasta under cold water to stop the cooking process and then drain it well in a colander. Otherwise, it is important *not* to rinse pasta, because it makes it difficult for the sauce to adhere and may wash away some of the nutrients.

One pound of uncooked pasta will produce up to 8 cups of cooked pasta. Most of the recipes in this book call for 1 pound of pasta to yield 4 main-course servings. As a first course, 1 pound of pasta would serve 6 to 8 people, depending on the dish.

Dried pasta should be stored sealed in a cool dry place, where it will keep for up to a year. For best retention of nutrients, dried pasta should not be exposed to light. Fresh pasta keeps well refrigerated for several days or frozen for up to a month.

About Beans

Many of the recipes in this book call for beans of one kind or another. Many people prefer to cook with dried beans, while others enjoy the convenience of canned. For that reason, my recipes invariably call for "cooked or canned" beans. You can decide whether to cook them on your own from scratch or not. If you're using canned beans, you may want to buy an organic variety, as they generally contain no additives. Be sure rinse canned beans in cold water and drain them before using. A drained 16-ounce can of beans is approximately equal to $1^1/_2$ cups in volume. For added convenience, the amount of beans used in these recipes is primarily $1^1/_2$ cups, to allow for canned beans to be easily used.

Dried beans need to be soaked prior to cooking. They can be quick-soaked in a pot of hot, boiled water for an hour, or left covered in the refrigerator to soak overnight. I like to add a piece of kombu seaweed to the pot when cooking beans: While it won't affect the taste, kombu acts as a natural flavor enhancer and tenderizer, and helps decrease the cooking time. It also adds important minerals and aids in digestion.

COOKING BEANS

To cook dried beans, simmer them over low heat in about 3 cups of water per 1 cup of beans. Cook with the lid on, stirring occasionally. Generally, 1 cup of dried beans will yield 2 to $2^1/_2$ cups of cooked beans. Cooking times may vary depending on the type, quality, and age of the bean, the altitude, and even the water quality.

BEAN COOKING CHART

Use this chart as a guideline for dried soaked beans cooked on the stovetop. Note that lentils and split peas do not require soaking prior to cooking.

BEAN (1 CUP DRIED)	WATER	COOKING TIME
Adzuki beans	3 cups	50 minutes
Black beans	3¹/₂ cups	1¹/₂–2 hours
Black-eyed peas	3 cups	1 hour
Cannellini beans	3¹/₂ cups	1¹/₂–2 hours
Chickpeas	4 cups	3 hours
Great Northern beans	3¹/₂ cups	1¹/₂–2 hours
Kidney beans	3¹/₂ cups	2 hours
Lentils	3 cups	35–45 minutes
Navy beans	3¹/₂ cups	1¹/₂–2 hours
Pinto beans	3¹/₂ cups	2 hours
Split peas	3 cups	45 minutes

Tofu, Tempeh, and Seitan

In addition to beans, the other primary plant-based protein sources are tofu (soybean curd), tempeh (compressed soybeans), and seitan (wheat-meat). Here is some basic information about each.

TOFU: Tofu is a curd made from soybeans. Its distinct lack of flavor makes tofu a valuable ingredient for the imaginative cook because it readily absorbs other flavors and seasonings. In years past, tofu was one of the few vegetarian protein choices available, but now, with the new meat alternatives in the spotlight, I tend to use tofu more as an egg or dairy substitute, although extra-firm tofu is wonderful in stir-fries and similar recipes. Before using tofu, drain it well and press out the water. Nutritionally, tofu is very high in protein, calcium, iron, and B-complex vitamins.

TEMPEH: Tempeh is fermented, compressed soybeans that are formed into firm cakes. Tempeh has a distinctive flavor and chewy texture and can be cubed, crumbled, or grated to resemble ground meat. It is high in protein and B vitamins, including vitamin B_{12}. Tempeh can be found in the refrigerated section of natural foods stores and some supermarkets. For best results, I recommend that you poach tempeh before using it to mellow out the flavor of the tempeh and also make it more digestible. When recipes call for "poached tempeh," it simply means that you need to simmer the tempeh in water for 15 minutes before using in the recipe. To do this, place the tempeh in a saucepan with enough water to cover and bring to a boil. Reduce the heat to medium and simmer for 15 minutes. Drain the tempeh and set aside to cool, then use as directed.

SEITAN: Called "wheat-meat" because it is made from wheat, seitan (pronounced "say-TAN") can be used in virtually any meat recipe. It can be ground, diced, cubed, or sliced. Made with wheat flour and water, seitan can be purchased in several forms, including a dry "quick mix." Ready-made seitan is also available in jars or in the frozen-food or refrigerated sections of most natural foods stores. In addition to being a good source of protein, vitamin C, and iron, seitan is also low in fat and calories: One 4-ounce serving contains only 70 calories and 1 gram of fat.

Other Meat Alternatives

Beyond beans, tofu, tempeh, and seitan are a number of commercially available products that mimic meats in taste and texture. Usually a blend of soy and grains, these products can be extremely helpful to the creative cook trying to please a diverse crowd. From meatless sausage to ground beef alternatives, it's now a simple matter to transform most any "meat" recipe into a healthful meatless version. Just like different cuts of meat, each of these meat alternatives lends different subtleties of taste and texture to a recipe.

One of the best products available in terms of taste, texture, and ease of use is the frozen cooked ground beef substitute. It tastes remarkably like ground beef but is low in fat and cholesterol-free. These vegetable protein "crumbles" are sold under a variety of brand names and are available in the freezer sections of many supermarkets and natural foods stores. Most of them come "precooked" or already browned and ready to use. Two brands, Boca Recipe Crumbles and

Morningstar Farms Burger-Style Recipe Crumbles, are available in most supermarkets. Both come in 12-ounce packages, which is equivalent to about 1 pound of uncooked ground beef. Other products exist that may need to be lightly cooked before using, so, for the sake of clarity, the recipes in this book specify the use of a "cooked" ground beef alternative and refer to the types of product brands mentioned above.

Dairy Alternatives

A wide variety of dairy alternatives available in supermarkets and natural foods stores can be used interchangeably with dairy products in these recipes.

Soy milk, as well as rice, oat, almond, or coconut milk can be used to replace cow's milk in cooking. Eggless mayonnaise, nondairy sour cream, cream cheese, and yogurt are all available made from soy.

There are a number of soy cheeses available as well, from grated soy Parmesan and shredded soy mozzarella to soy cheddar and Monterey Jack, available sliced, shredded, and in blocks. Because of its salty, cheese-like flavor, some people also like to use nutritional yeast as a cheese alternative.

Instead of butter, you can opt for nonhydrogenated margarine. To replace eggs in recipes, use Ener-G Egg Replacer, an egg replacement powder made from vegetable starch. You can find this in natural foods stores, and it is easy to use in recipes. Other egg alternatives include tofu and ground flax seeds blended with water until the mixture becomes viscous.

About Vegetable Stock

The use of vegetable stock to make soups and stews is a matter of personal taste. While it isn't always necessary to a recipe, it does add nutrients and an extra dimension of flavor. Making vegetable stock is not difficult, nor does it need to be time consuming. It can be as easy as boiling water—all you have to do is add some vegetables to the water and walk away. After about an hour of simmering, you can strain out the vegetables, and the resulting liquid is your stock. Cook it longer, and the stock is richer.

An all-purpose vegetable stock made with little more than onions, carrots, celery, and water is a modest investment that will provide dividends to your meals. When I make vegetable stock, I begin by sweating the vegetables in a little oil to deepen their flavors. I usually coarsely chop the vegetables, often keeping the skins, peels, stems, and leaves on for added taste. Just be sure that all ingredients are well washed before adding them to the pot. Many of the soup or stew recipes in this book call for stock or water. In these cases, water will work just fine in the recipe, but using stock will enrich the flavor; the choice is yours.

When there's no time to make homemade stock, but you want a more complex flavor than you would achieve with water, you can buy canned vegetable broth or use vegetable bouillon cubes or powdered vegetable soup base as a quick and easy substitute. These products vary in saltiness, so experiment to find ones you like, and remember to adjust the seasonings in your recipes accordingly. Sometimes when I don't have stock, I will add a splash of tamari or a little bit of dissolved miso paste to enrich the flavor of a dish.

The actual amount of salt you add to a stock is up to you, but less is better than more. While salt does help bring out the flavor of the vegetables, adding too much salt will impair the flavor, especially if the stock is reduced further, which will intensify the saltiness. I usually begin with 1 teaspoon of salt, then adjust the seasoning toward the end, after the flavors have had a chance to develop.

Use this basic vegetable stock as a guideline. Feel free to add other vegetables or seasonings according to personal preference, although it is best to omit boldly colored or strongly flavored vegetables that will overpower the stock.

Vegetable Stock

1 tablespoon extra virgin olive oil

1 large yellow onion, coarsely chopped

2 celery ribs, chopped

2 carrots, coarsely chopped

8 cups water

2 garlic cloves, crushed

½ cup coarsely chopped fresh Italian parsley

1 large bay leaf

½ teaspoon whole black peppercorns

1 tablespoon tamari

Salt to taste

1 Heat the oil in a large stockpot over medium heat. Add the onion, celery, and carrots, cover, and cook until slightly softened, about 5 minutes. Uncover and add the water, garlic, parsley, bay leaf, peppercorns, tamari, and salt. Bring to a boil, then reduce the heat to medium-low and simmer, uncovered, for 1 hour to reduce the liquid and bring out the flavors of the vegetables.

2 Strain through a fine-mesh sieve into another pot, pressing the juices out of the vegetables with the back of a large spoon. Discard the vegetables. The stock is now ready to use. If a stronger stock is desired, return the stock to a boil, and reduce the volume by one quarter. If kept tightly covered in the refrigerator, the stock will keep for up to 3 days. Alternatively, you can portion and freeze it for up to 4 months.

MAKES ABOUT 6 CUPS

About Oils

I generally recommend keeping at least three varieties of oil on hand: extra virgin olive oil for salads and most cooking, toasted sesame oil for added flavor to certain Asian dishes, and a light-flavored oil such as safflower oil (which is very low in saturated fat) for cooking at higher temperatures or when you don't want the flavor of olive oil or sesame oil. High-quality, cold-pressed oils are always the best choice.

About Chiles and Chili Powder

Since there is an entire chapter in this book devoted to chili, a few words about chiles and chili powder seem in order. These days, many supermarkets carry a selection of both fresh and dried chiles, so experimenting can be fun. When handling chiles, it is best to wear rubber gloves, being careful not to touch your eyes as the capsaicin oil will burn. Some of the hotter chiles even release fumes that are quite strong. Always wash your hands and gloves thoroughly in warm soapy water after handling chiles.

You can make your own chili powder blend using already ground dried chiles or dried whole chiles that you can grind yourself; customize the blend by adding cumin and other seasonings such as oregano and paprika.

Commercially available chili powders are generally a blend of ground chile peppers combined with cumin, oregano, garlic, and salt. These blends vary greatly in quality and flavor and can sometimes be stale or of inferior quality. In selecting a commercial powder blend, try to find one that consists only of ground chiles, oregano, and cumin. For the best flavor, try to steer clear of those containing garlic, salt, and other additives.

The following recipe is one of my favorite blends; you can use it anytime a recipe calls for "chili powder," as your preference for hot or mild dictates.

Use this as a guideline and experiment with different types and amounts of chiles to create your own signature blend. The other spice amounts may be adjusted as well.

Medium Hot Chili Powder

2 dried cayenne chiles, stems and seeds removed

2 dried ancho chiles, stems and seeds removed

2 dried Anaheim chiles, stems and seeds removed

1 tablespoon cumin seeds

1 tablespoon paprika

1 teaspoon dried oregano, preferably Mexican

Cut the chiles into small pieces and place in a blender or spice mill. Add the cumin, paprika, and oregano and grind into a fine powder. Store in an airtight container in a cool, dry place.

NOTE: If you prefer to begin with ground spices, here is a good ratio to start with, adjusting for hotter or milder, to taste: Combine 1 cup mild ground dried chiles, 1/4 cup hot ground dried chiles, 2 tablespoons ground cumin, and 2 tablespoons ground oregano.

MAKES ABOUT 1 1/2 CUPS

Other Ingredients

Because the recipes in this book are inspired by numerous global cuisines, there may be some ingredients that you have never tried. Most of the ingredients used in these recipes can be found in any well-stocked supermarket. In the case of any unusual ingredient, I've tried to list an alternative choice in case the first choice is unavailable in your location.

Like most health-conscious people, I believe that fresh, organic ingredients are best and that highly processed food is to be avoided. You will notice that many of the recipes call for tamari instead of regular soy sauce. This is because tamari does not contain the additives found in many brands of soy sauce. I also recommend sea salt over regular table salt and favor natural sweeteners over sugar.

Recipe Yields and Portion Amounts

Deciding how many people a certain recipe will serve can be tricky. After all, we don't all eat the same amount at meals—some people have large appetites while others prefer smaller portions. Factor in that the recipes may be served alone or with other dishes, and it is clear that the yield amount is a guideline and not a hard-and-fast rule. Because this book is designed for "one-dish meals," the yield amounts lean to larger portions, the assumption being that the recipe in question is the meal itself, perhaps with a salad, bread, or other accompaniment. Most of the recipes in this book yield four servings. However, if you know that your family tends to eat smaller portions, or if you plan to serve a few other dishes or courses with a particular recipe, then you may be able to stretch six or more portions out of a recipe designed to feed four hearty appetites as a one-dish meal.

Healthy Eating

A well-balanced, plant-based diet that includes lots of grains, beans, vegetables, and fruits continues to be a wise choice for healthy eating. And while many vegetarian cookbooks still call for dairy products, the trend toward healthy eating is moving away from the use of dairy products, owing to their high fat and cholesterol content as well as concern over ingesting pesticides, antibiotics, and other additives that can be found in milk.

In addition, many medical studies recommend that we eat more soy products; the USDA suggests that eating 25 grams of soy protein per day can reduce the risk of heart disease. As a result, more people are searching for delicious ways to enjoy tofu and other soy products. To that end, I feel it is important to make my recipes accessible to everyone—from health-conscious meat-eaters to vegetarians to vegans, as well as those who are lactose intolerant or who need to monitor their cholesterol intake. For that reason, in addition to being meatless, the recipes in this book are "dairy optional"—that is, I provide dairy-free, or vegan, options for each recipe that lists dairy as an ingredient.

Pantry Postscript

If you enjoy the convenience and ease of preparing one-dish meals, then a well-stocked pantry can be a valuable asset. When your larder is full of the ingredients used in these recipes, you'll never again be stumped at dinnertime.

Include a range of dried or canned beans such as chickpeas, cannellini beans, lentils, kidney beans, and pintos. Stock your pantry with a variety of pasta, rice, and other grains, extra virgin olive oil, and canned tomato products, including paste, puree, and diced and whole tomatoes. Keep on hand a supply of dried herbs, spices, sea salt, and other basic seasonings, as well as standard baking items such as flours, baking soda, baking powder, and extracts.

Line your shelves with olives, capers, sun-dried tomatoes, artichoke hearts, dried mushrooms, and roasted red peppers. For those times when you want to cook with an Asian flair, be sure to include tamari, toasted sesame oil, chili paste, fresh ginger, and other flavor enhancers.

A well-stocked kitchen should also include fresh staples such as onions, carrots, and celery, fresh lettuce and other salad ingredients, and a wide selection of vegetables and fruits, including fresh herbs when available.

By keeping a variety of basic ingredients on hand, you'll always be ready to create nourishing and flavorful meals whenever you want them.

SOUPS

AND

STEWS

Overflowing with juicy mushroom slices, this soup has a rich, complex flavor that belies its ease of preparation.

Thyme-Scented Mushroom-Rice Soup

1 tablespoon extra virgin olive oil

2 leeks (white parts only), chopped

1 celery rib, including leaves, chopped

1 cup long-grain white rice

5 cups Vegetable Stock (page 11) or water

2 tablespoons dry white wine

1 tablespoon minced fresh thyme or
   1 teaspoon dried

1 bay leaf

12 ounces white mushrooms, sliced
   (about 3 cups)

2 tablespoons minced fresh Italian parsley

Salt and freshly ground black pepper to
   taste

1   Heat the oil in a large saucepan over medium heat. Add the leeks and celery and cook, stirring occasionally, until softened, about 5 minutes. Add the rice, stock, wine, the dried thyme, if using, and the bay leaf, bring to a simmer, and simmer for 15 minutes.

2   Stir in the mushrooms, parsley, and the fresh thyme, if using. Season with salt and pepper and cook for 10 minutes longer, or until the rice is tender. Remove the bay leaf and serve hot.

SERVES 4

I usually use Wehani for its deep flavor, or a short-grain brown rice for its chewy texture in this hearty soup, but you can use any variety of rice. Adding rice to minestrone makes a nice change from pasta.

Minestrone with Rice

1 tablespoon extra virgin olive oil

1 medium-size onion, minced

2 carrots, diced

2 garlic cloves, minced

8 ounces green beans, ends trimmed and cut into 2-inch pieces

2 zucchini, diced

One 14.5-ounce can diced tomatoes, drained

8 cups water

1 bay leaf

1 tablespoon minced fresh basil or 1 teaspoon dried

1 teaspoon minced fresh oregano or $1/2$ teaspoon dried

$1/2$ teaspoon minced fresh thyme or $1/4$ teaspoon dried

$1^{1}/2$ to 2 cups cooked or canned cannellini beans, rinsed and drained if canned

1 teaspoon salt

$1/8$ teaspoon freshly ground black pepper

$1^{1}/2$ cups cooked short-grain brown, Wehani, or other rice

$1/4$ cup minced fresh Italian parsley

1   Heat the oil in a large stockpot over medium heat. Add the onion, carrots, and garlic and cook, stirring frequently, for about 5 minutes, or until the vegetables begin to soften. Add the green beans, zucchini, tomatoes, water, bay leaf, and the dried basil, oregano, and thyme, if using, and bring to a boil. Reduce the heat and simmer for 30 minutes or until the liquid reduces slightly and the vegetables are soft.

2   Add the cannellini beans, salt, and pepper and simmer for 10 minutes. Adjust the seasonings as desired and remove the bay leaf.

3   Stir in the cooked rice, parsley, and the fresh basil, oregano, and thyme, if using, heat through, and serve hot.

SERVES 4 TO 6

Since gumbo is actually an African word for okra, the name of this recipe may seem redundant. But with a hearty soup this delicious, why mince words? Be sure to place a bottle of Tabasco sauce on the table so your guests can spice up their gumbo to their liking. Although some versions of gumbo are made with just a small amount of rice, I prefer it thick with rice and served as a more substantial stew-like dish. The filé powder, made from ground sassafras leaves, helps to thicken this.

Okra Gumbo

1 tablespoon extra virgin olive oil

1 medium-size onion, diced

1 green bell pepper, diced

1/2 cup chopped celery

2 garlic cloves, minced

6 cups water

One 14.5-ounce can diced tomatoes, drained

1 1/2 cups sliced fresh or frozen okra

1/2 teaspoon filé powder

1 teaspoon dried thyme

1 teaspoon salt, or to taste

1/4 teaspoon freshly ground black pepper, or to taste

1/8 teaspoon cayenne pepper

1 1/2 cups cooked or canned kidney beans, rinsed and drained if canned

3 to 4 cups hot cooked white, Texmati, or other long-grain rice

1 Heat the oil in a large saucepan over medium heat. Add the onion, bell pepper, celery, and garlic, cover, and cook, stirring occasionally, for 5 minutes, or until soft. Remove the cover, add the water, tomatoes, okra, filé powder, thyme, salt, black pepper, and cayenne and bring to a simmer. Simmer over low heat, stirring occasionally, for 30 minutes.

2 Add the beans and simmer 5 to 10 minutes longer to heat through. Taste and adjust the seasoning. Place the rice in soup bowls and ladle the hot gumbo over it.

SERVES 4

Miso is a rich Japanese soybean paste that is said to have many healing properties. Be sure not to boil the soup once the miso paste has been added, since boiling destroys valuable enzymes. Long- or short-grain brown rice would be a good choice here for maximum nutritional benefits.

Shiitake Miso Soup

5 cups water

4 ounces shiitake mushrooms, stemmed and sliced (about 1 cup)

1/2 cup chopped scallions

1/4 cup finely shredded carrots

1/2 teaspoon minced fresh ginger

1 tablespoon tamari

3 tablespoons miso paste

1 cup chopped fresh spinach leaves

1 cup cooked long- or short-grain brown rice

4 ounces firm silken tofu, drained, blotted dry, and diced

1 Bring the water to a boil in a medium saucepan over high heat. Add the mushrooms, scallions, carrots, ginger, and tamari, reduce the heat to medium, and simmer for 10 minutes, or until the vegetables soften.

2 Reduce the heat to low. Transfer about 1/4 cup of the hot soup to a small bowl and add the miso paste, blending well. Stir the blended miso into the soup along with the chopped spinach and simmer for 2 minutes, being careful not to boil. Divide the rice and tofu among 4 soup bowls and ladle the hot soup into the bowls.

SERVES 4

Peanut butter and coconut milk blend harmoniously with ginger, lime juice, and chiles in a sublime soup made substantial with the last-minute addition of cooked rice. A fragrant jasmine or basmati would complement the delightful flavor and aroma of this soup. Kecap manis, a sweet, thick soy sauce, is available at Asian markets.

Indonesian Peanut Soup

1 tablespoon peanut oil

1 medium-size onion, chopped

1 red bell pepper, chopped

2 garlic cloves, minced

1 small hot chile, seeded and minced

1 tablespoon minced fresh ginger

1/2 cup chunky peanut butter

1 cup unsweetened coconut milk

2 tablespoons kecap manis

1 tablespoon fresh lime juice

4 to 5 cups water

2 cups cooked rice, preferably basmati or jasmine

Salt and freshly ground black pepper to taste

1/4 cup chopped peanuts, for garnish

1   Heat the oil in a large saucepan over medium heat. Add the onion, bell pepper, garlic, chile, and ginger and cook, stirring occasionally, until soft, about 5 minutes. One at a time, stir in the peanut butter, coconut milk, kecap manis, lime juice, and water, blending well after each addition. Bring to a simmer and simmer for 15 to 20 minutes, until the vegetables are tender and the flavors are well blended.

2   Reduce the heat to low, add the rice, and season with salt and pepper. Simmer for 5 minutes or until heated through. Serve hot, sprinkled with the chopped peanuts.

SERVES 4

Homemade vegetable soup in less than 30 minutes? I put this soup together when I'm short on time and ingredients but crave a vegetable soup with a rich, simmered-for-hours flavor. I use whatever rice I happen to have on hand—leftover wild rice medley is especially tasty. Add a cup of cooked beans for additional substance and protein.

Vegetable Rice Soup

1 tablespoon extra virgin olive oil

1 large onion, chopped

2 carrots, chopped

1/2 cup chopped celery

1 garlic clove, minced

6 cups water

2 tablespoons tamari

2 teaspoons vegetable bouillon granules or 2 bouillon cubes

1 cup frozen peas

Salt and freshly ground black pepper to taste

2 cups cooked rice

1 tablespoon minced fresh Italian parsley, for garnish

1   Heat the oil in a large saucepan over medium heat. Add the onion, carrots, celery, and garlic, cover, and cook, stirring occasionally, until softened, about 5 minutes. Add the water, tamari, and vegetable bouillon and bring to a simmer, then reduce the heat to low and simmer until the vegetables are tender, about 15 minutes.

2   Add the peas and salt and pepper and gently cook 5 minutes longer. Stir in the rice and heat through, then ladle into bowls. Garnish with the parsley.

SERVES 4

Delicate grains of jasmine rice absorb this flavorful broth, hot with chiles and tangy with lemongrass, ginger, and lime juice.

Hot Thai Soup

6 cups water

1 teaspoon salt

3 lemongrass stalks, cut into 1-inch lengths

2 serrano chiles, thinly sliced

1 teaspoon slivered fresh ginger

1 cup canned sliced bamboo shoots, rinsed and drained

$1/2$ cup unsweetened coconut milk

1 tablespoon tamari

Juice of 1 lime

2 cups cooked jasmine rice

$1/4$ cup coarsely chopped fresh Thai basil, for garnish

1   In a large saucepan, combine the water, salt, lemongrass, chiles, and ginger. Bring to a boil, then reduce the heat and simmer for 20 minutes.

2   Strain the broth through a sieve, return it to the saucepan, and boil for 2 minutes. Reduce the heat to low and add the bamboo shoots, coconut milk, tamari, and lime juice. Stir well and simmer for 5 minutes. Place $1/2$ cup of rice in the bottom of each bowl, ladle the soup over the rice, sprinkle with the basil leaves, and serve hot.

SERVES 4

Rice is used to thicken as well as to enrich this warming winter soup. Very soft rice works best, so if your cooked rice is on the firm side, add it to the pot as the vegetables are simmering to cook it a little longer.

Creamy Winter Vegetable Soup

1 tablespoon extra virgin olive oil

1 medium-size onion, diced

1 carrot, chopped

1/4 cup minced celery

1 Yukon Gold or other potato, peeled and diced

1 cup diced butternut squash

1 garlic clove, minced

1/2 teaspoon dried marjoram

5 cups water

2 cups cooked white or brown rice

Salt and freshly ground black pepper to taste

Minced fresh Italian parsley or chives, for garnish

1   Heat the oil in a large saucepan over medium heat. Add the onion, carrot, and celery and cook, covered, for 5 minutes, or until softened. Add the potato, squash, garlic, marjoram, and water, bring to a simmer, and simmer for 20 minutes, or until the vegetables are tender. Stir in the cooked rice and remove from the heat.

2   Puree the soup mixture, in batches, in a food processor until smooth and return to the saucepan. Reheat slowly over low heat, stirring occasionally. Season with salt and pepper and serve sprinkled with the parsley or chives.

SERVES 4

Wild rice and woodsy mushrooms are a natural combination, and the touch of thyme enhances the rich flavors in this simple but elegant soup. The watercress is added near the end of the cooking time so it retains its fresh taste and vivid color.

White and Wild Watercress Soup

1 tablespoon extra virgin olive oil

1 medium-size onion, minced

2 celery ribs, minced

1/2 cup wild rice

8 cups Vegetable Stock (page 11) or water

1 teaspoon salt

1/8 teaspoon cayenne pepper

1 tablespoon chopped fresh thyme or 1 teaspoon dried

1 bay leaf

1/2 cup long-grain white rice

1 cup diced mushrooms, preferably shiitake (stemmed), cremini, or other exotic mushrooms

2 bunches watercress, tough stems removed and chopped

1   Heat the oil in a large saucepan over medium heat. Add the onion and celery and cook until softened, about 5 minutes. Stir in the wild rice, add the stock, salt, and cayenne, and bring to a boil. Reduce the heat to low, add the dried thyme, if using, and the bay leaf, cover, and simmer for 40 minutes.

2   Add the white rice and mushrooms and simmer for 20 minutes longer.

3   Stir in the watercress and the fresh thyme, if using, and cook for 5 minutes, or until the rice is tender. Taste and adjust the seasoning, discard the bay leaf, and serve hot.

SERVES 4 TO 6

Inspired by the classic curried soups of Senegal, this uses rice both as a thickener and to mellow out the flavorful seasonings. Garnish with chopped peanuts or golden raisins.

Senegalese-Style Curried Soup

1 tablespoon safflower oil

1 large onion, chopped

$^1/_2$ cup chopped celery

1 Granny Smith apple, peeled and chopped

$1^1/_2$ tablespoons curry powder

$^1/_2$ teaspoon salt

$^1/_4$ teaspoon cayenne pepper

About 4 cups Vegetable Stock (page 11) or water

$1^1/_2$ cups cooked long- or short-grain white rice

Chopped peanuts or golden raisins, for garnish

1   Heat the oil in a large saucepan over medium heat. Add the onion and celery and cook for 5 minutes, or until the vegetables are soft. Stir in the apple, curry powder, salt, cayenne, and $3^1/_2$ cups of the stock and bring to a boil. Add the rice and simmer, stirring occasionally, for 15 minutes, or until the rice is very soft.

2   Transfer the soup to a food processor, in batches if necessary, and puree. Pour into a large bowl and whisk in as much of the remaining stock or water as necessary to achieve the desired consistency. Refrigerate for 2 hours, or until cold. Serve the soup chilled, garnished with peanuts or raisins.

SERVES 4

Nearly every Friday when I was a child, I'd come home from school to find a pot of "pasta fazool" simmering on the stove. To this day, whenever I make this popular pasta and bean soup, a flood of memories comes rushing back.

Pasta Fagioli

2 tablespoons extra virgin olive oil

1 medium-size onion, minced

1 large garlic clove, minced

One 6-ounce can tomato paste

¼ teaspoon dried oregano

1 bay leaf

6 cups Vegetable Stock (page 11) or water

Salt and freshly ground black pepper to taste

8 ounces elbow or small-shell macaroni

3 cups cooked or canned red kidney beans or canellini beans, rinsed and drained if canned

Freshly grated Parmesan or soy Parmesan cheese, for garnish

1   Heat the oil in a large pot over medium heat. Add the onion and cook for 5 to 7 minutes or until soft. Add the garlic and cook for 1 minute. Reduce the heat to low and blend in the tomato paste. Add the oregano, bay leaf, stock, and salt and pepper and simmer over low heat for about 30 minutes.

2   Meanwhile, cook the macaroni in a large pot of salted boiling water, stirring occasionally, until it is just *al dente*. Drain.

3   When the 30 minutes are up, stir the beans and the pasta into the soup. Simmer gently for 10 minutes to blend the flavors. Remove the bay leaf, ladle the soup into bowls, and serve hot, passing the grated cheese at the table.

SERVES 4 TO 6

In both Milan and Genoa, a swirl of pesto is added near the end of cooking time to enrich this classic soup. If you prefer, instead of adding the cooked pasta to the soup pot, you can place a large spoonful into the bottom of the soup bowls at serving time, and ladle the hot soup over the tiny pasta.

Minestrone with Pesto

2 tablespoons extra virgin olive oil

3 garlic cloves, minced

1 large onion, minced

2 carrots, cut into 1/4-inch slices

1/2 small cabbage, shredded

1 medium-size potato, diced

One 14.5-ounce can diced tomatoes, drained

2 tablespoons tomato paste

7 cups Vegetable Stock (page 11) or water

1 teaspoon dried basil

1/2 teaspoon dried oregano

Salt and freshly ground black pepper to taste

1 1/2 cups cooked or canned cannellini beans, rinsed and drained if canned

1 zucchini, thinly sliced

4 ounces green beans, ends trimmed and cut in half (about 1 cup)

1/2 cup anellini or ditalini pasta

2 tablespoons chopped fresh Italian parsley

1/2 cup prepared pesto

1 Heat the oil in a large stockpot over medium heat, and add the garlic, onion, carrots, and cabbage. Cook, stirring, for about 10 minutes. Add the potato, tomatoes, tomato paste, stock, basil, oregano, and salt and pepper. Bring the mixture to a boil, reduce the heat, and simmer for 30 minutes.

2 Stir in the cannellini beans, zucchini, and green beans and cook for another 20 minutes.

3 Meanwhile, cook the pasta in a large pot of salted boiling water, stirring occasionally, until it is *al dente*. Drain and stir it into the soup along with the parsley. Simmer gently for 10 minutes to blend the flavors. Ladle the soup into bowls and top with a swirl of pesto.

SERVES 4 TO 6

Some version of minestrone or other hearty soup is eaten on a daily basis throughout Southern Italy, usually as the evening meal. Calabria, located at the "toe of the boot," is no exception. The inclusion of yellow bell peppers is typically Calabrese.

Starstruck Minestrone with Yellow Peppers and Chickpeas

2 tablespoons extra virgin olive oil

1 large onion, minced

1 carrot, chopped

1 large yellow bell pepper, chopped

1 celery rib, including leaves, chopped

3 garlic cloves, minced

One 14.5-ounce can diced tomatoes, drained

7 cups Vegetable Stock (page 11) or water

1 bay leaf

1 teaspoon fresh savory, or
1/2 teaspoon dried

1 teaspoon fresh marjoram, or
1/2 teaspoon dried

Salt and freshly ground black pepper to taste

1 pound fresh spinach, coarsely chopped

1 1/2 cups cooked or canned chickpeas, rinsed and drained if canned

2 tablespoons chopped fresh Italian parsley

1/2 cup stellini or acini di pepe pasta

Freshly grated Parmesan or soy Parmesan cheese, for garnish

1   Heat the oil in a large stockpot over medium heat. Add the onion, carrot, bell pepper, celery, and garlic and cook until soft, about 10 minutes. Add the tomatoes, stock, bay leaf, savory, marjoram, and salt and pepper. Bring to a boil, reduce the heat, and simmer for 30 minutes.

2   Add the spinach, chickpeas, and parsley and cook another 15 minutes.

3   Meanwhile, cook the stellini in a large pot of salted boiling water, stirring occasionally, until it is *al dente*. Drain and stir it into the soup. Simmer gently for 5 to 10 minutes to blend the flavors. Remove the bay leaf, ladle the soup into bowls, and top with freshly grated cheese.

SERVES 4 TO 6

The people of Tuscany are known as "bean eaters" owing to the popularity of legumes in their cooking. In addition to the creamy cannellini bean, Tuscans favor chickpeas, favas, and borlotti beans, which are also known as cranberry or Roman beans.

Tuscan White Bean Soup with Ditalini

1 tablespoon extra virgin olive oil

1 medium-size onion, minced

1 celery rib, minced

1 large garlic clove, minced

1/4 cup tomato paste

One 14.5-ounce can diced tomatoes, drained

1 1/2 cups cooked or canned cannellini beans, rinsed and drained if canned

1/2 teaspoon salt, or to taste

Cayenne pepper to taste

1/4 teaspoon dried oregano

7 cups Vegetable Stock (page 11) or water

8 ounces ditalini pasta

Freshly grated Parmesan or soy Parmesan cheese, for garnish

1   Heat the oil in a stockpot over medium heat. Add the onion and celery and cook until soft, about 5 minutes. Add the garlic and cook for 30 seconds. Blend in the tomato paste. Add the diced tomatoes, beans, salt, cayenne, oregano, and stock. Simmer over low heat for 30 minutes.

2   Meanwhile, cook the ditalini in a large pot of salted boiling water, stirring occasionally, until it is *al dente*. Drain and stir it into the soup. Simmer gently for 10 minutes to blend the flavors. Ladle the soup into bowls, sprinkle with cheese, and serve immediately.

SERVES 4 TO 6

The name origin of many Italian foods is associated with colorful stories, and tortellini is no exception. According to legend, tortellini was created by a Bolognese innkeeper who was so inspired by Venus that he shaped the pasta to resemble her navel. This soup may also be made with chicory or spinach in place of the escarole, if you prefer.

Tortellini Escarole Soup

1 tablespoon extra virgin olive oil

1 medium-size onion, chopped

2 carrots, chopped

1 large garlic clove, crushed

1 head escarole, coarsely chopped

6 cups Vegetable Stock (page 11) or water

1½ cups cooked or canned cannellini beans, rinsed and drained if canned

½ teaspoon dried marjoram

Salt and freshly ground black pepper to taste

1 cup small, dried cheese tortellini

1   Heat the oil in a large stockpot over medium heat. Add the onion, carrots, and garlic and cook, covered, for 5 minutes to soften the vegetables. Add the escarole and stock and simmer for 15 minutes. Stir in the beans, marjoram, and salt and pepper. Simmer for 15 more minutes.

2   Meanwhile, cook the tortellini in a large pot of salted boiling water according to package directions until just tender. When the pasta is cooked, drain it and add to the hot soup just before serving.

SERVES 4 TO 6

Tiny acini di pepe are so named because they resemble peppercorns. For a smoother, more elegant texture, pass the soup through a food mill or fine mesh strainer before combining it with the pasta.

Tomato-Basil Soup with "Peppercorn" Pasta

1 tablespoon extra virgin olive oil

1 medium-size onion, chopped

1/4 cup minced celery

2 garlic cloves, crushed

2 tablespoons tomato paste

3 cups Vegetable Stock (page 11) or water

Two 28-ounce cans crushed plum tomatoes

1/4 teaspoon red pepper flakes

1 bay leaf

Salt and freshly ground black pepper to taste

1/2 cup acini di pepe pasta

1/3 cup minced fresh basil

1   Heat the oil in a large stockpot over medium heat. Add the onion and celery. Cover and cook until softened, about 5 minutes. Add the garlic and cook 1 minute longer. Stir in the tomato paste. Add the stock, tomatoes, red pepper flakes, and bay leaf and bring to boil. Season with salt and pepper. Reduce the heat to low and simmer for 30 minutes, stirring occasionally. Adjust the seasonings as desired and remove the bay leaf.

2   Meanwhile, cook the pasta in a large pot of salted boiling water until it is tender. Drain and add it to the soup just prior to serving, along with the fresh basil.

SERVES 4 TO 6

Although chard is often called "Swiss" chard after a Swiss botanist, it is actually a Mediterranean vegetable. Nutrient-rich chard and lentils combine for a healthful wintertime soup with a rich complex flavor.

Lentil Soup with Chard and Orzo

2 tablespoons extra virgin olive oil

1 medium-size onion, minced

1 carrot, grated

1/2 cup minced celery

2 garlic cloves, minced

7 cups Vegetable Stock (page 11) or water

1 cup dried brown lentils, rinsed and picked over

2 tablespoons tomato paste

1/2 cup dry red wine

1/2 cup minced fresh Italian parsley

1/2 teaspoon minced fresh thyme or 1/4 teaspoon dried

Salt and freshly ground black pepper to taste

2 cups coarsely chopped Swiss chard

1/2 cup orzo

1   Heat the oil in a stockpot over medium heat. Add the onion, carrot, celery, and garlic. Cover and cook for 5 minutes. Add the stock, lentils, tomato paste, wine, parsley, thyme, and salt and pepper. Bring to a boil, then reduce the heat and simmer for about 20 minutes, stirring occasionally. Stir in the chard and simmer for another 10 minutes, stirring occasionally, until the lentils are tender.

2   Meanwhile, cook the orzo in a large pot of salted boiling water, stirring occasionally, until it is *al dente*. Drain and stir the orzo into the hot soup, then ladle it into bowls and serve immediately.

SERVES 4 TO 6

This comforting soup can be altered easily to suit your taste. For example, vary the vegetables according to personal preference, add a can of chickpeas or other beans for extra substance and protein, or spice it up with a pinch of red pepper flakes.

Vegetable Noodle Soup

8 ounces fettuccine

2 tablespoons extra virgin olive oil

1 medium-size onion, chopped

2 carrots, cut into ½-inch dice

7 cups Vegetable Stock (page 11) or water

4 ounces green beans, ends trimmed and cut into 1-inch pieces (1 cup)

3 cups coarsely chopped green cabbage

One 14.5-ounce can diced tomatoes, drained

1 tablespoon minced fresh Italian parsley

Salt and freshly ground black pepper to taste

½ cup frozen peas

1   Break the fettuccine into 3- to 4-inch pieces and cook in a large pot of salted boiling water, stirring occasionally, until it is *al dente*. Drain and place it in a bowl. Add 1 tablespoon of the oil, toss to combine, and set aside.

2   In a large stockpot, heat the remaining tablespoon of oil over medium-high heat. Add the onion and carrots. Cover and cook until the vegetables soften, 5 to 7 minutes. Remove the cover and add the stock, green beans, cabbage, tomatoes, parsley, and salt and pepper. Simmer for 20 minutes or until the vegetables are tender and the liquid reduces slightly.

3   Stir in the peas and fettuccine. Simmer for 5 minutes to blend the flavors before ladling the soup into bowls and serving hot.

SERVES 4 TO 6

The porcini mushrooms and dry vermouth add depth to the delicate broth in this soup. Look for frozen tofu ravioli in natural foods stores. I like to serve this as a light but elegant entrée preceded by a substantial appetizer such as black olive bruschetta, accompanied by a dry white wine, and finished with a rich dessert.

Ravioli in Leek and Mushroom Essence

2 tablespoons extra virgin olive oil

1 leek (white part only), minced

4 ounces porcini mushrooms, thinly sliced (about 1 cup)

6 cups Vegetable Stock (page 11)

2 tablespoons dry vermouth

Salt and freshly ground black pepper to taste

1 pound frozen tofu or cheese ravioli

1 tablespoon chopped fresh chives, for garnish

1 Heat 1 tablespoon of the oil in a large stockpot over medium heat. Add the leek and cook until softened, about 4 minutes. Add the mushrooms and cook until slightly softened, about 2 minutes longer. Add the stock and vermouth, and bring to a boil. Reduce the heat to low and simmer until the liquid reduces by about 1 cup, about 20 minutes. Strain the broth through a fine-mesh strainer into a saucepan, reserving the leek and mushroom solids.

2 In a small skillet, heat the remaining tablespoon of oil over medium heat. Add the leek and mushroom solids, cook for 1 minute, season with salt and pepper, and keep warm over low heat.

3 Cook the ravioli in a large pot of salted boiling water according to the package directions. Drain, divide among individual shallow bowls, and surround with the hot broth. Top with a spoonful of the mushroom and leek mixture and sprinkle with chives. Serve immediately.

SERVES 4

Linguine noodles and shiitake mushrooms swim in a broth flavored with ginger and a hint of sesame oil in this Asian-flavored soup. Once the miso paste has been added to the broth, be sure it does not return to a boil, as boiling will destroy the beneficial enzymes in the miso.

Noodle Soup in Shiitake-Ginger Broth

8 ounces linguine

1 teaspoon toasted sesame oil

6 cups Vegetable Stock (page 11) or water

4 ounces shiitake mushrooms, thinly sliced
(about 1 cup)

1 tablespoon minced fresh ginger

1 bunch scallions, finely minced

2 tablespoons tamari

1 tablespoon white miso paste

1 tablespoon minced fresh Italian parsley,
for garnish

1   Cook the linguine in a large pot of boiling salted water until it is *al dente*. Drain and place it in a bowl. Add the sesame oil, toss to coat the pasta, and set aside.

2   Bring the stock to a boil in a large saucepan with the mushrooms, ginger, scallions, and tamari. Reduce the heat to low and simmer for 5 minutes or until the shiitakes soften.

3   Blend the miso paste with $1/4$ cup of the hot broth in a small bowl. Stir the miso mixture into the soup, add the linguine, sprinkle with parsley, and serve immediately.

SERVES 4

This stew relies on a cornucopia of fresh vegetables for its texture and flavor. It's a great way to make sure everyone eats their vegetables.

Garden Vegetable Stew

1 tablespoon extra virgin olive oil

1 large onion, chopped

1 large carrot, diced

1 small red bell pepper, diced

1/2 cup chopped celery

2 garlic cloves, minced

1 jalapeño chile, seeded and minced

2 small zucchini, diced

2 large tomatoes, chopped

2 cups fresh or frozen corn kernels

2 cups water

One 6-ounce can tomato paste

1 teaspoon salt

1 teaspoon dried oregano

1 teaspoon sugar

2 tablespoons minced fresh Italian parsley, for garnish

Heat the oil in a large stockpot over medium heat. Add the onion, carrot, bell pepper, celery, garlic, and jalapeño. Cover, and cook, stirring occasionally, until the vegetables begin to soften, about 10 minutes. Add the zucchini, tomatoes, corn, water, tomato paste, salt, oregano, and sugar and stir well. Bring to a boil, lower the heat, and simmer until the vegetables are tender, about 30 minutes, adding more water if necessary. Serve garnished with the minced parsley.

SERVES 4

Brightly colored vegetables add visual appeal as well as flavor and texture to this recipe. Vary the vegetables according to your taste.

Veggie Confetti Stew

1 tablespoon extra virgin olive oil

1 cup chopped red onion

2 medium-size carrots, diced

2 garlic cloves, minced

1 small green bell pepper, diced

1 small red bell pepper, diced

1 small sweet potato, peeled and diced

2 cups fresh or frozen corn kernels

2 cups diced tomatoes, fresh or canned

One 6-ounce can tomato paste

1 teaspoon ground cumin

1 teaspoon salt

2 cups Vegetable Stock (page 11) or water

1 1/2 cups cooked or canned pinto beans, rinsed and drained if canned

1 1/2 cups cooked or canned Great Northern beans or other white beans, rinsed and drained if canned

Heat the oil in a large stockpot over medium heat. Add the onion, carrots, and garlic. Cover and cook until softened, about 5 minutes. Add the bell peppers, sweet potato, corn, tomatoes, tomato paste, cumin, salt, and stock to the pot and stir to combine. Bring to a boil, stirring frequently. Lower the heat and simmer, covered, for 30 minutes, or until the vegetables are tender. Add the pinto beans and the Great Northern beans and simmer, uncovered, 15 minutes longer to heat through and thicken. Serve hot.

SERVES 4 TO 6

The rich, mellow flavor of roasted root vegetables makes this a perfect choice for a late autumn meal, accompanied by warm, fresh bread. As with all vegetables, be sure to thoroughly wash the carrots, parsnips, and potato. Even if they are well scrubbed, you may want to peel them also, unless they are organic.

Roasted Root Vegetable Stew

2 tablespoons extra virgin olive oil

1 large onion, chopped

2 large carrots, diced

2 parsnips, diced

1 large potato, diced

Salt and freshly ground black pepper to taste

1 garlic clove, minced

1 jalapeño chile, minced

One 6-ounce can tomato paste

2 cups water

3 cups cooked or canned pinto beans, rinsed and drained if canned

1 Preheat the oven to 400°F. Spread 1 tablespoon of the oil in the bottom of a shallow baking pan.

2 Distribute the onion, carrots, parsnips, and potato in the pan and toss to coat them with oil. Sprinkle the vegetables with salt and pepper, and place the pan in the oven. Roast the vegetables until softened and slightly browned, about 30 minutes, turning them over once.

3 Meanwhile, heat the remaining oil in a large stockpot over medium heat. Add the garlic and jalapeño and cook until fragrant, about 3 minutes. Add the tomato paste, water, and salt to taste and stir well. Bring to a boil, lower the heat, cover, and simmer for 20 minutes to blend the flavors.

4 Add the roasted vegetables to the pot along with the pinto beans and simmer 15 minutes longer. Serve hot.

SERVES 4

Lentils are popular in the United States, as well as in Europe, India, and the Middle East. They are rich in calcium, potassium, zinc, and iron. This lentil stew makes great company fare—not too hot, but full of flavor. Accompaniments might include separate bowls of crushed peanuts, golden raisins, and chutney.

Tomato-Lentil Stew over Couscous

2 tablespoons extra virgin olive oil

1 large onion, chopped

1 carrot, chopped

1 red bell pepper, chopped

2 garlic cloves, minced

1 cup dried brown lentils, rinsed and picked over

One 28-ounce can crushed tomatoes

1 bay leaf

1 teaspoon salt

1 teaspoon dried marjoram

2 cups tomato juice

3 cups Vegetable Stock (page 11) or salted water

1½ cups couscous

2 tablespoons minced scallions

2 tablespoons minced fresh Italian parsley or cilantro

1   Heat the oil in a large pot over medium heat. Add the onion, carrot, bell pepper, and garlic. Cover and cook until the onion is softened, about 5 minutes. Add the lentils and enough water to cover the lentils by 1 inch. Bring to a boil, lower the heat, and simmer, covered, for 30 minutes, or until the lentils are tender.

2   Add the tomatoes, bay leaf, salt, marjoram, and tomato juice and simmer for 15 minutes, stirring occasionally. If the mixture becomes too dry, add a small amount of water. (Be sure to remove the bay leaf from the stew before serving.)

3   While the stew is simmering, prepare the couscous. Bring the 3 cups stock to a boil in a medium saucepan. Add the couscous and 1 tablespoon each of the scallions and parsley, cover, and remove the pan from the heat. Allow the couscous to sit for 5 minutes. Serve the couscous in a shallow bowl or serving dish, with the stew on top. Garnish with the remaining scallions and parsley.

SERVES 4

MAIN-DISH

SALADS

A basket of warm cornbread would make a good accompaniment for this south-of-the-border salad. Choose long-grain white rice for a striking color contrast or brown rice to add a slightly nutty flavor to the dish.

Black Bean and Avocado Rice Salad

1 teaspoon minced lime zest

3 tablespoons fresh lime juice

1 tablespoon cider vinegar

2 tablespoons fresh orange juice

1/2 teaspoon minced garlic

1 teaspoon light brown sugar

1/2 teaspoon chili powder

1/2 teaspoon salt

1/8 teaspoon cayenne pepper

1/3 cup extra virgin olive oil

2 ripe Hass avocados

1 tablespoon fresh lemon juice

3 cups cold cooked long-grain white or brown rice

1 1/2 cups cooked or canned black beans, rinsed and drained if canned

1 small red onion, chopped

One 4-ounce can diced mild green chiles, drained

Torn romaine lettuce leaves, for serving

12 cherry tomatoes, halved, for garnish

1   In a small bowl, whisk together the lime zest, lime juice, vinegar, orange juice, garlic, brown sugar, chili powder, salt, and cayenne. Whisk in the oil in a slow, steady stream until emulsified and smooth. Set aside.

2   Peel and pit the avocados, cut into 1/2-inch dice, and toss with the lemon juice.

3   In a large bowl, combine the rice, beans, onion, chiles, and avocados. Add the dressing and toss gently to combine. Line plates or shallow bowls with lettuce leaves and top with the salad. Garnish with the cherry tomatoes and serve.

SERVES 4

Garlic, fresh herbs, and roasted red peppers imbue this salad with full-bodied Mediterranean flavors. Use roasted red peppers packed in oil for ease of preparation. Grated fennel adds a slightly sweet taste and a fresh-tasting crunch.

Mediterranean Rice Salad with Roasted Red Peppers

2 tablespoons balsamic vinegar

1 tablespoon fresh lemon juice

2 garlic cloves, minced

1 tablespoon minced fresh basil or
　　1 teaspoon dried

1/2 teaspoon minced fresh oregano or
　　1/4 teaspoon dried

1/2 teaspoon salt

1/8 teaspoon freshly ground black pepper

1/3 cup extra virgin olive oil

3 cups cold cooked brown basmati or
　　other rice

1/2 cup grated fresh fennel

1/2 cup chopped red onion

1 1/2 cups cooked or canned chickpeas,
　　rinsed and drained if canned

One 4-ounce jar roasted red peppers,
　　drained and chopped

Torn mixed salad greens, for serving

Oil-cured black olives, pitted, for garnish

1　In a small bowl, whisk together the vinegar, lemon juice, garlic, basil, oregano, salt, and pepper. Whisk in the oil in a slow, steady stream until emulsified and smooth. Set aside.

2　In a large bowl, combine the rice, fennel, onion, chickpeas, and roasted red peppers. Add the dressing and toss well. Cover and refrigerate for at least 30 minutes before serving.

3　Line a platter with salad greens and top with the rice salad. Garnish with the black olives and serve.

SERVES 4

The combination of brown rice and adzuki beans is a protein-rich mainstay of a macrobiotic diet. Adzuki beans are small red Japanese beans that can be found canned or dried in natural foods stores. Whenever I eat this salad, I feel energized by the healthful combination of ingredients.

Brown Rice and Adzuki Bean Salad

3 cups cooked long-grain brown rice

1½ cups cooked or canned adzuki beans, rinsed and drained if canned

1 cucumber, peeled, halved lengthwise, seeded, and diced

¼ cup minced scallions

¼ cup minced fresh Italian parsley

1½ cups coarsely chopped watercress (tough stems removed)

3 tablespoons rice wine vinegar

1 tablespoon tamari

1 tablespoon fresh lemon juice

1 teaspoon minced fresh ginger

½ teaspoon salt

⅛ teaspoon freshly ground black pepper

3 tablespoons toasted sesame oil

2 tablespoons safflower oil

1 In a large bowl, combine the rice, beans, cucumber, scallions, parsley, and watercress.

2 In a small bowl, whisk together the vinegar, tamari, lemon juice, ginger, salt, and pepper. One at a time, gradually add both oils in a slow, steady stream, whisking constantly until emulsified and smooth.

3 Pour the dressing over the rice mixture and toss gently to coat the rice. Serve in a shallow bowl.

SERVES 4

The surprising crunch of apple and walnuts in this vibrant, luscious dish inspired by the classic Waldorf salad will make this a favorite addition to the buffet table. Fragrant basmati rice lends an extra touch of sweetness.

Waldorf Rice Salad

1 large Red Delicious or Granny Smith apple

2 tablespoons fresh lemon juice

3 cups cold cooked basmati rice

3/4 cup raisins

3/4 cup finely chopped celery

1/2 cup chopped walnuts

1/4 cup minced scallions

1/2 cup mayonnaise or soy mayonnaise

1 teaspoon Dijon mustard

2 tablespoons cider vinegar

1 teaspoon sugar

1/2 teaspoon salt

2 tablespoons safflower oil

Lettuce leaves, for serving

1   Cut the apple into 1/2-inch dice and place in a large bowl. Add the lemon juice and toss to coat. Add the rice, raisins, celery, walnuts, and scallions. Set aside.

2   In a small bowl, whisk together the mayonnaise, mustard, vinegar, sugar, and salt. Whisk in the oil in a slow, steady stream, until emulsified and smooth. Add the dressing to the salad and mix gently to combine. Cover the salad and refrigerate for at least 30 minutes before serving.

3   To serve, line a shallow bowl or individual plates with lettuce leaves and mound the salad on top.

SERVES 4

Put this fresh-tasting tarragon-kissed salad together in the morning so it's ready for a no-fuss dinner on a hot summer night. It's especially good served with focaccia, the savory Italian flatbread. If you prefer another fresh herb to the fragrant tarragon, feel free to use it instead.

Cannellini Beans and Rice with Lemon-Tarragon Vinaigrette

$^1\!/_2$ cup minced red onion

$^1\!/_2$ cup minced celery

$1^1\!/_2$ to 2 cups cooked or canned cannellini beans, rinsed and drained if canned

2 large ripe tomatoes, seeded and chopped

3 cups cold cooked long-grain rice

1 small garlic clove, minced

$^1\!/_4$ cup minced fresh tarragon

2 tablespoons minced fresh Italian parsley

1 teaspoon salt

$^1\!/_4$ teaspoon freshly ground black pepper

3 tablespoons fresh lemon juice

2 tablespoons white wine vinegar

$^1\!/_4$ teaspoon sugar

$^1\!/_2$ cup extra virgin olive oil

Torn mixed salad greens, for serving

1   In a large bowl, combine the onion, celery, beans, tomatoes, and rice. Set aside.

2   In a food processor, combine the garlic, tarragon, parsley, salt, and pepper and process to mince very finely. Add the lemon juice, vinegar, and sugar. With the machine running, gradually add the olive oil in a slow, steady stream, processing until emulsified and smooth. Add enough of the dressing to the rice mixture to coat, tossing gently to combine. Let stand for 30 minutes.

3   To serve, in a large bowl, toss the greens with the remaining dressing. Place the greens in a large shallow serving bowl and mound the rice salad in the center.

SERVES 4

This salad is a great way to use up leftover wild rice, but we enjoy it so much that I usually keep cooked wild rice in the freezer so I can put it together on a whim. Vary the vegetables according to your own preference and availability. Leftover cooked vegetables also make welcome additions.

Wild About Rice Salad

3 cups cold cooked long-grain white or brown rice

1 cup cold cooked wild rice

1/4 cup cider vinegar

1/2 teaspoon salt

1/8 teaspoon freshly ground black pepper

1/2 cup extra virgin olive oil

1 yellow or red bell pepper, chopped

1/2 cup frozen peas, thawed

1/4 cup minced scallions

1/4 cup minced fresh Italian parsley

Torn mixed salad greens, for serving

1   Place both rices in a large bowl and set aside.

2   In a small bowl, whisk together the vinegar, salt, and pepper. Add the oil in a slow, steady stream, whisking constantly until emulsified and smooth. Pour the dressing over the rice and toss to coat it with the dressing. Add the bell pepper, peas, scallions, and parsley and toss gently to combine. Taste and adjust the seasoning. Serve on a bed of mixed salad greens.

SERVES 4

Brown basmati rice adds substance to this slightly sweet salad, inspired by the popular carrot and raisin combination found at many salad bars.

Carrot and Raisin Rice Salad with Cashews

3 cups cold cooked brown basmati rice

2 large carrots, finely shredded

3/4 cup golden raisins

1/4 cup chopped scallions

1 tablespoon fresh lemon juice

1/2 cup fresh orange juice

1/4 teaspoon ground cinnamon

1/4 teaspoon ground allspice

1/2 teaspoon salt

1/8 teaspoon freshly ground black pepper

1/4 cup safflower oil

Boston lettuce leaves, for serving

1/2 cup chopped cashews, for garnish

1 In a large bowl, combine the rice, carrots, raisins, and scallions. Set aside.

2 In a small bowl, whisk together the lemon juice, orange juice, cinnamon, allspice, salt, and pepper. Add the oil in a slow, steady stream, whisking constantly until emulsified and smooth. Pour the dressing over the salad and toss gently to combine. Cover the salad and refrigerate for at least 1 hour before serving.

3 To serve, line a shallow serving bowl with lettuce leaves, mound the salad in the center, and garnish with the cashews.

SERVES 4

You could make a quicker version of this salad using a prepared three-bean salad, but I like the fresher taste offered by assembling my own, using just-cooked green beans. If fresh wax beans are in season, you could substitute them for the chickpeas.

Three-Bean Rice Salad

8 ounces green beans, ends trimmed and cut into 1-inch pieces (2 cups)

1 1/2 cups cooked or canned kidney beans, rinsed and drained if canned

1 1/2 cups cooked or canned chickpeas, rinsed and drained if canned

1 cucumber, peeled, halved lengthwise, seeded, and diced

1/4 cup diced pimientos

2 tablespoons minced fresh Italian parsley

1/4 cup fresh lemon juice

1 teaspoon minced garlic

1 teaspoon dry mustard

1/2 teaspoon salt

1/8 teaspoon freshly ground black pepper

1/2 cup extra virgin olive oil

3 cups cold cooked long-grain rice

Torn mixed salad greens, for serving

Sliced ripe tomatoes, for serving

1 Steam the green beans over boiling water until just tender, about 5 minutes. Run under cold water to stop the cooking process and retain the color; drain well.

2 In a large bowl, combine the three beans, the cucumber, pimientos, and parsley. Set aside.

3 In a small bowl, whisk together the lemon juice, garlic, mustard, salt, and pepper. Add the oil in a slow, steady stream, whisking constantly until emulsified and smooth. Pour the dressing over the bean mixture and toss to coat. Let stand, covered, at room temperature for 20 to 30 minutes.

4 Drain the excess dressing from the bean mixture over a bowl, add the rice, and toss to combine. Taste and adjust the seasoning, adding some of the reserved dressing if desired. Serve the salad in shallow bowls lined with salad greens, topped with tomato slices.

SERVES 4

Classic *salade niçoise* ingredients team up with penne pasta for a great-tasting Mediterranean fusion salad that's perfect for warm-weather *al fresco* dining.

Chilled Pasta Niçoise

1 pound penne

1/2 cup extra virgin olive oil

8 ounces green beans, ends trimmed and blanched

1 1/2 cups cooked or canned cannellini beans, rinsed and drained if canned

1 cup cherry tomatoes, halved

1/2 cup niçoise olives, pitted

1/4 cup minced fresh Italian parsley

1/4 cup white wine vinegar

1 garlic clove, crushed

2 teaspoons Dijon mustard

1/2 teaspoon salt

Freshly ground black pepper to taste

Torn mixed salad greens, for serving

1   Cook the penne in a large pot of salted boiling water, stirring occasionally, until it is *al dente*. Drain, rinse under cold water, and place in a large bowl. Toss with 1 tablespoon of the oil and add the green beans, cannellini beans, tomatoes, olives, and parsley.

2   To make the dressing, combine the vinegar, garlic, mustard, salt, and pepper in a small bowl. Whisk in the remaining oil and add to the pasta and vegetables. Toss gently to combine. Taste to adjust the seasonings if necessary. Divide the salad greens among individual plates, top with the pasta salad, and serve.

SERVES 4

Baked marinated tofu is available in the refrigerated section of well-stocked supermarkets and natural foods stores. If unavailable, rinsed canned chickpeas or other beans may be added instead. This is a fun salad to adapt for holiday gatherings. For example, at Christmastime, use red and green peppers and add some broccoli florets and cherry tomatoes. For Halloween, use orange and black bell peppers and toss in some grated carrots, black olives, and black beans.

Three-Pepper Pasta Salad

1 pound fusilli

1/2 cup extra virgin olive oil

1 green bell pepper

1 red bell pepper

1 yellow bell pepper

8 ounces baked marinated tofu, cut into 1/2-inch dice

1/4 cup red wine vinegar

1 garlic clove, crushed

2 tablespoons minced fresh Italian parsley

Salt and freshly ground black pepper to taste

Torn mixed salad greens, for serving

1   Cook the fusilli in a large pot of salted boiling water, stirring occasionally, until it is *al dente*. Drain, rinse under cold water, and place in a large serving bowl. Toss with 1 tablespoon of the oil and set aside.

2   Halve and seed the bell peppers and place on a baking sheet, skin side up. Place under the broiler until the skins are blackened. Place the peppers in a plastic or paper bag and let stand for about 10 minutes. Remove the charred skin from the peppers and cut into thin strips. Add to the pasta along with the tofu.

3   To make the dressing, combine the vinegar, garlic, parsley, and salt and pepper in a small bowl. Whisk in the remaining oil and blend well. Add the dressing to the pasta and toss gently to combine. Serve on top of salad greens on individual plates or in a large shallow serving bowl.

SERVES 4

The flavors of ratatouille, the classic French vegetable mélange, are well suited to pair with pasta. This salad is delicious served at room temperature, making it perfect for a buffet. However, I usually serve it warm for a seated meal. Either way, a crisp salad and warm, crusty bread are good accompaniments.

Ratatouille Radiatore

1 pound radiatore

1/2 cup extra virgin olive oil

1 small eggplant, cut into 1/2-inch dice

2 small zucchini, halved lengthwise and sliced

12 ounces white mushrooms, thinly sliced (about 3 cups)

Salt and freshly ground black pepper to taste

6 ripe plum tomatoes, coarsely chopped

1/4 cup minced fresh Italian parsley

1 tablespoon capers

2 garlic cloves, crushed

3 tablespoons red wine vinegar

2 tablespoons chopped fresh basil leaves

1   Cook the radiatore in a large pot of salted boiling water, stirring occasionally, until it is *al dente*. Drain, and rinse under cold water. Place in a large serving bowl, toss with 1 tablespoon of the oil, and set aside.

2   Heat 1 tablespoon of the oil in a skillet over medium heat. Add the eggplant, cover, and cook until softened, about 5 minutes. Stir in the zucchini, mushrooms, and salt and pepper and cook until just softened, about 5 minutes. Stir in the tomatoes, parsley, and capers and transfer to a bowl.

3   To make the dressing, combine the garlic, vinegar, and salt and pepper to taste in a small bowl. Whisk in the remaining oil and pour the dressing over the vegetables. Let the vegetables marinate at room temperature for 30 minutes, then add to the pasta, along with the basil. Taste to adjust the seasonings and serve at room temperature.

SERVES 4

Evocative of a summer day, seashell and butterfly pastas combine with broccoli florets and sunflower seeds for a whimsical ray of sunshine any time of year.

Summer Sunshine Pasta Salad

8 ounces farfalle

1/4 teaspoon ground turmeric

8 ounces small shell pasta

1/3 cup plus 1 tablespoon extra virgin
  olive oil

2 cups broccoli florets, blanched

Juice and zest of 1 orange

2 tablespoons fresh lemon juice

Salt to taste

Cayenne pepper to taste

1 yellow bell pepper, cut into thin strips

1 1/2 cups cooked or canned chickpeas,
  rinsed and drained if canned

1 small red onion, chopped

1 cup cherry tomatoes, halved

1/4 cup sunflower seeds

1 Cook the farfalle in a large pot of salted boiling water, stirring occasionally, until it is *al dente*. While the farfalle is cooking, add the turmeric to the water to turn the pasta bright yellow. Cook the pasta shells in a separate pot of salted boiling water until they are *al dente*. When both pastas are cooked, drain and rinse under cold water. Place both pastas in a bowl, toss with 1 tablespoon of the oil, add the broccoli, and set aside.

2 To make the dressing, combine the orange juice and zest, lemon juice, salt, and cayenne in a small bowl. Whisk in the remaining oil until blended, then pour the dressing over the pasta. Add the bell pepper, chickpeas, onion, and tomatoes and toss to combine. Sprinkle on the sunflower seeds before serving.

SERVES 4

Ruote, sometimes called rotelle, is shaped like the wagon wheels of the Old West—a fitting choice for this taste of the Southwest.

Cumin-Spiced Pasta Salad with Jalapeño Pesto

1/3 cup plus 2 tablespoons extra virgin olive oil

1 teaspoon ground cumin

12 ounces ruote pasta

1 small red onion, chopped

2 jalapeño chiles, halved and seeded

1 large garlic clove

1 1/2 cups cooked or canned pinto beans, rinsed and drained if canned

1/2 cup coarsely chopped fresh Italian parsley

2 tablespoons fresh lime juice

1 teaspoon brown sugar

1/2 teaspoon chili powder

Salt to taste

Torn mixed salad greens, for serving

1   Heat 2 tablespoons of the oil in a skillet over medium heat. Add the cumin and stir until fragrant, about 30 seconds. Set aside.

2   Cook the pasta in a large pot of salted boiling water, stirring occasionally, until it is *al dente*. Drain, rinse under cold water, and place in a bowl. Add the cumin–olive oil mixture and onion, toss to combine, and set aside.

3   In a food processor, pulse the jalapeños and garlic until minced. Add the beans, parsley, lime juice, brown sugar, chili powder, and salt. With the machine running, pour the remaining oil through the feed tube and process to a smooth paste. Add the jalapeño pesto to the pasta and toss to coat. To serve, divide the pasta salad among plates lined with salad greens.

SERVES 4

With bottled salsa and canned pinto beans, this south-of-the-border salad can be put together in minutes. Serve with warm cornbread and some cold Mexican beer.

Pinto Bean and Salsa Pasta Toss with Lime and Avocado

12 ounces rotini

1½ cups cooked or canned pinto beans, rinsed and drained if canned

2 cups salsa, store-bought or homemade (page 81)

2 tablespoons minced fresh cilantro

Salt to taste

2 ripe Hass avocados, peeled, pitted, and cut into ½-inch dice

Juice and zest of 1 lime

2 tablespoons extra virgin olive oil

Cayenne pepper to taste

Torn mixed salad greens, for serving

1   Cook the rotini in a large pot of salted boiling water, stirring occasionally, until it is *al dente*. Drain, rinse under cold water, and place in a large bowl. Add the beans, salsa, and cilantro and toss to combine. Season with salt.

2   To make the dressing, combine the avocados, lime juice and zest, oil, cayenne, and salt to taste in a small bowl. Toss gently to coat the avocados with lime juice. To serve, divide the pasta salad among individual plates lined with salad greens, top with avocado dressing, and serve.

SERVES 4

Long thin shreds of papaya and carrot look best in this refreshing salad. Make them yourself with a mandoline slicer or look for them in the produce section of well-stocked Asian markets. Those with milder tastes may cut down on or eliminate the red pepper flakes. However, hot food lovers might prefer substituting fresh minced Thai bird's eye chiles for a jolt of extra-fiery heat.

Lime-Dressed Vermicelli with Green Papaya and Peanuts

12 ounces vermicelli

1/3 cup toasted sesame oil

Juice and zest of 1 lime

2 garlic cloves, minced

2 tablespoons rice wine vinegar

2 teaspoons grated fresh ginger

1 teaspoon light brown sugar

1/4 teaspoon red pepper flakes, or to taste

Salt to taste

1 green papaya, shredded

1 carrot, shredded

4 scallions, minced

1/2 cup chopped peanuts

1   Cook the vermicelli in a large pot of salted boiling water, stirring occasionally, until it is *al dente*. Drain, rinse under cold water, and place in a large serving bowl. Add 1 tablespoon of the sesame oil, toss to combine, and set aside.

2   To make the dressing, combine the remaining oil, the lime juice and zest, garlic, vinegar, ginger, brown sugar, red pepper flakes, and salt in a small bowl. Add the papaya, carrot, scallions, and dressing to the pasta and toss together. Sprinkle with chopped peanuts before serving.

SERVES 4

Tofu adds substance to this refreshing Asian-inspired salad. Look for baked marinated tofu in well-stocked supermarkets and natural foods stores. If unavailable, dice and bake or sauté plain extra-firm tofu and season it with tamari.

Spicy Cucumber Pasta Salad

12 ounces linguine

1/4 cup plus 1 tablespoon toasted sesame oil

2 cucumbers, peeled and halved lengthwise

1 bunch scallions, minced

8 ounces baked marinated tofu, cut into 1/2-inch dice

1 teaspoon Asian chili paste, or to taste

Juice and zest of 2 limes

1 teaspoon sugar

Salt to taste

1/4 cup minced fresh cilantro or basil

1   Cook the linguine in a large pot of salted boiling water, stirring occasionally, until it is *al dente*. Drain, rinse under cold water, and place in a large serving bowl. Add 1 tablespoon of the sesame oil, toss to combine, and set aside.

2   Seed the cucumber halves, cut them into 1/2-inch slices, and add to the pasta along with the scallions and tofu. To make the dressing, combine the remaining oil, the chili paste, lime juice and zest, sugar, and salt in a small bowl. Pour the dressing over the pasta and cucumbers, sprinkle with cilantro, and toss gently to combine.

SERVES 4

Quality ingredients are the key to this summertime favorite. Be sure to use extra virgin olive oil and only the freshest, ripest tomatoes. This easy sauce is terrific served with either hot or cold pasta, and it makes a good addition to a potluck since it doesn't need to be kept warm.

Fusilli with Uncooked Tomato Sauce

2 pounds ripe tomatoes, coarsely chopped (about 4 cups)

1 garlic clove, minced

¼ cup extra virgin olive oil

¼ cup chopped fresh basil

Salt and freshly ground black pepper to taste

1 pound fusilli

Freshly shaved Parmesan or soy Parmesan cheese, for garnish

1   Place the tomatoes in a large bowl. Add the garlic, oil, basil, and salt and pepper. Stir gently to combine. Cover, and let stand at room temperature for 30 to 45 minutes to allow the flavors to blend. Stir occasionally.

2   Meanwhile, cook the fusilli in a large pot of salted boiling water, stirring occasionally, until it is *al dente*. Drain and place in a shallow serving bowl. Add the sauce and toss gently to combine. Serve immediately, or, if serving cold, refrigerate until close to serving time, but allow to come to room temperature before serving. Top with a few shavings of cheese, passing additional cheese separately.

SERVES 4

Not to be outdone by the Italians, the Lebanese have their own delicious bread salad, which they make with stale pita bread. I use whole wheat pita for added flavor and nutrition. The addition of chickpeas and tahini is a departure from the traditional, but they add lots of protein and turn this refreshing salad into a one-dish meal.

Fattoush (Lebanese Bread Salad)

2 garlic cloves, mashed into a paste

2 teaspoons tahini (sesame paste)

1/3 cup fresh lemon juice

1/3 cup extra virgin olive oil

1/2 teaspoon salt

Pinch of cayenne pepper

2 large or 4 small white or whole wheat pita breads

1 large cucumber, peeled, seeded, and chopped

1 large ripe tomato, seeded and chopped

1/2 small green bell pepper, seeded and chopped

1/2 cup minced red onion

1 1/2 cups cooked or canned chickpeas, rinsed and drained if canned

1/3 cup chopped fresh Italian parsley leaves

1/3 cup chopped fresh mint leaves

2 cups shredded romaine lettuce

1 Preheat the oven to 350°F.

2 In a small bowl, whisk together the garlic, tahini, lemon juice, olive oil, salt, and cayenne until blended. Set aside.

3 Place the pitas on a baking sheet and bake until lightly toasted, turning once, 10 to 12 minutes. Remove from the oven, cut or tear into bite-size pieces, and place in a large bowl. Add the cucumber, tomato, bell pepper, onion, chickpeas, parsley, mint, and as much of the dressing as needed to coat. Toss well to combine, then let sit for 10 to 15 minutes to let the flavors develop.

4 Divide the lettuce among 4 salad plates, top with the salad, and serve.

SERVES 4

This classic Middle Eastern salad is normally made with bulgur, tomato, and loads of chopped parsley and mint. Here it is given a new twist with quinoa, the protein-rich "super grain" of the Incas, and yellow tomatoes, although red tomatoes may be substituted if yellow are unavailable. Be sure to rinse the quinoa well before using to remove the bitter white coating called saponin. Fresh cilantro replaces the mint, and the optional tiny red adzuki beans can be added for substance. These mild-tasting, highly digestible beans are available dried or canned at natural foods stores.

Quinoa Tabbouleh

1 cup quinoa

2 cups water

Salt to taste

2 medium-size ripe yellow tomatoes, seeded and chopped

1/4 cup minced red onion

1/2 cup cooked or canned adzuki beans (optional), rinsed and drained if canned

Leaves from 1 bunch fresh Italian parsley, minced

3 tablespoons chopped fresh cilantro leaves

1/3 cup extra virgin olive oil

2 tablespoons fresh lemon juice

Freshly ground black pepper to taste

1 Wash the quinoa thoroughly to remove any trace of the bitter white coating, then rinse and drain.

2 Bring the water to a boil in a medium-size saucepan. Add salt and the quinoa. Reduce the heat to low, cover, and simmer until all the water is absorbed, about 15 minutes. Blot the quinoa with paper towels to remove excess moisture.

3 Place the quinoa in a large serving bowl and set aside to cool. Add the tomatoes, onion, the adzuki beans, if using, parsley, and cilantro.

4 In a small bowl, whisk together the olive oil, lemon juice, and salt and pepper until blended. Pour the dressing over the salad and toss well to combine.

5 Cover and refrigerate for at least 1 hour before serving. For the best flavor, this salad should be served the day it is made. Serve chilled.

SERVES 4

Sweet ripe tomatoes combine with creamy white beans and refreshing crisp watercress for a lovely salad combination that tastes as good as it looks. Add a loaf of warm crusty bread, and you have a delicious light meal.

Tomato and White Bean Salad with Watercress

2 shallots

1 garlic clove

2 tablespoons fresh lemon juice

1 teaspoon Dijon mustard

1/4 cup extra virgin olive oil

Salt and freshly ground black pepper to taste

1 1/2 cups cooked or one 15-ounce can cannellini or other white beans, rinsed and drained if canned

2 bunches watercress, tough stems removed and coarsely chopped

12 grape or cherry tomatoes, halved

8 brine-cured black olives, pitted

2 tablespoons chopped fresh basil leaves

1 Place the shallots and garlic in a food processor and process until smooth. Add the lemon juice, mustard, olive oil, and salt and pepper. Process until well blended and set aside.

2 In a large serving bowl, combine the beans, watercress, tomatoes, olives, and basil. Pour the dressing over the salad and toss gently to combine. Serve immediately.

SERVES 4

BAKED

DISHES

The nutty flavor and cohesive texture of short-grain brown rice work well in this stuffing. Zucchini can be substituted for the yellow squash, or use two of each kind of squash.

Rice-Stuffed Summer Squash

4 yellow squash, halved lengthwise and seeded

2 cups cooked short-grain brown, jasmine, or other rice

2 tablespoons minced onion

2 tablespoons minced green bell pepper

2 tablespoons minced fresh Italian parsley

1/2 cup firm tofu, drained, blotted dry, and crumbled

3 tablespoons freshly grated Parmesan or soy Parmesan cheese

1/2 teaspoon salt

1/8 teaspoon cayenne pepper

1   Bring a large pot of water to a boil, add the squash halves, and blanch for 1 to 2 minutes. Drain and set aside.

2   Preheat the oven to 350°F. Lightly oil a large baking dish.

3   In a large bowl, combine the rice, onion, bell pepper, parsley, tofu, cheese, salt, and cayenne, mixing well. Spoon the stuffing into the squash halves and arrange them in the baking dish. Bake until the squash is tender and the stuffing is lightly browned, about 30 minutes. Serve hot.

SERVES 4

The rich flavor of these stuffed peppers is enhanced by the smoky sweetness of the sun-dried tomatoes. The rice mixture can also be used to stuff zucchini or other vegetables or enjoyed on its own.

Bell Peppers Stuffed with Rice, Spinach, and Sun-Dried Tomatoes

4 large green, red, or yellow bell peppers

1/2 cup sun-dried tomatoes packed in olive oil

1 tablespoon extra virgin olive oil

1 large bunch spinach, washed, trimmed, and coarsely chopped

1 garlic clove, minced

3 to 4 cups cooked long-grain white or brown rice

1 tablespoon minced fresh Italian parsley

1/4 teaspoon salt

1/8 teaspoon freshly ground black pepper

1 Preheat the oven to 350°F.

2 Slice off the tops of the bell peppers and remove the seeds and membranes. Plunge the peppers into a pot of boiling water and cook for 2 to 3 minutes, or until slightly softened. Remove the peppers from the water and set aside, cut side down, to drain. Chop the tomatoes and set aside.

3 Heat the oil in a large skillet over medium heat. Add the spinach, garlic, and tomatoes and cook until the spinach is wilted, 2 to 3 minutes. Add the rice, parsley, salt, and pepper and stir to combine. Fill the peppers with the rice mixture and place upright in a baking dish. Add a few tablespoons of water to the baking dish, cover, and bake until the filling is hot and the peppers are tender, 30 to 40 minutes. Serve hot.

SERVES 4

While paella generally includes meat and/or seafood, this vegetarian rendition brims with vegetables and derives its protein from meaty cannellini beans. Paella is traditionally made with Spanish Valencia rice, which can be found in specialty food shops. If unavailable, arborio rice may be substituted. In any case, use a short-grain rice for authenticity. The saffron is traditional, but turmeric can be used to create the same golden color at a fraction of the cost.

Vegetable Paella

2 tablespoons extra virgin olive oil

1 medium-size onion, chopped

1 red bell pepper, diced

8 ounces green beans, ends trimmed and cut into 1-inch pieces (2 cups)

One 28-ounce can plum tomatoes, drained and chopped

2 garlic cloves, finely chopped

4 cups Vegetable Stock (page 11) or water

1 1/2 cups Valencia or other short-grain rice

1/4 teaspoon ground fennel

Pinch of saffron threads or 1/4 teaspoon ground turmeric

1/2 teaspoon salt

1/2 teaspoon red pepper flakes

1 1/2 to 2 cups cooked or canned cannellini beans, rinsed and drained if canned

1 cup frozen peas, thawed

1   Preheat the oven to 375°F.

2   Heat the oil in a large ovenproof skillet or saucepan over medium heat. Add the onion, bell pepper, and green beans and cook for 5 minutes, or until softened. Stir in the tomatoes, garlic, and stock and bring to a boil, then stir in the rice, fennel, saffron, salt, and red pepper flakes. Remove from the heat, cover, and place in the oven. Bake for 30 to 40 minutes, or until the rice is tender.

3   Remove from the oven, stir in the cannellini beans and peas, cover, and let stand for 10 minutes before serving.

SERVES 4

Biryani, a classic dish of northern India, usually includes a variety of spices, vegetables, dried fruits, nuts, and basmati rice. It is traditionally baked as a layered casserole and makes a festive one-dish meal. Serve this fragrant dish with warmed naan bread and a spicy sweet chutney, available, along with the garam masala spice mixture, at Indian markets.

Vegetable Biryani

1 tablespoon safflower oil

1 medium-size onion, diced

1 green bell pepper, diced

8 ounces green beans, ends trimmed and cut into 1-inch pieces (2 cups)

1 carrot, thinly sliced

1 teaspoon minced fresh ginger

2 garlic cloves, minced

2 teaspoons garam masala, or to taste

1/2 teaspoon ground turmeric

1/2 teaspoon salt

1/4 teaspoon cayenne pepper

1 1/2 cups basmati rice

4 cups water

1 1/2 cups cooked or canned kidney beans, rinsed and drained if canned

Peanuts, for garnish

Raisins, for garnish

1   Preheat the oven to 375°F.

2   Heat the oil in a large ovenproof casserole over medium heat. Add the onion, bell pepper, green beans, and carrot and cook, stirring occasionally, until soft, about 10 minutes. Add the ginger, garlic, garam masala, turmeric, salt, and cayenne and cook for 2 minutes longer, stirring to combine. Stir in the rice, then stir in the water. Cover and bake for 30 minutes, or until the rice and vegetables are tender.

3   Remove from the oven, stir in the kidney beans, replace the lid, and let stand for 5 minutes. Serve directly from the casserole, sprinkled with peanuts and raisins.

SERVES 4

Two favorites—lasagne and eggplant Parmesan—are combined in one delicious dish. What could be better? You can use a good-quality bottled pasta sauce or make your own using the recipe on page 92. Instead of the regular lasagna noodles, you may substitute the ones that do not require precooking.

Eggplant Parmesan Lasagne

2 tablespoons extra virgin olive oil

1 eggplant, cut into 1/2-inch slices

8 ounces lasagna noodles

1 pound firm tofu, drained and blotted dry

1/2 cup freshly grated Parmesan or soy Parmesan cheese

3 tablespoons minced fresh Italian parsley

Salt and freshly ground black pepper to taste

3 cups tomato-based pasta sauce, store-bought or homemade

1 cup shredded mozzarella or soy mozzarella cheese

1   Preheat the oven to 350°F.

2   Heat the oil in a large skillet over medium heat, add the eggplant, and cook until lightly browned on both sides, about 5 minutes, cooking in batches if necessary. Transfer the eggplant to a large plate lined with paper towels and set aside.

3   Cook the lasagna noodles according to the package directions. While the pasta is cooking, crumble the tofu into a large bowl. Add 1/4 cup of the Parmesan, the parsley, and salt and pepper, and mix well.

4   Spread a layer of the pasta sauce in the bottom of a 9 x 13-inch baking dish. Top the sauce with a layer of noodles. Top the noodles with half of the eggplant, then spread half of the tofu mixture over the eggplant. Repeat with another layer of noodles, and top with more sauce. Repeat the layering process with the remaining eggplant mixture and the remaining tofu mixture, ending with a layer of noodles topped with sauce. Sprinkle the mozzarella and the remaining Parmesan on top. Bake for 45 minutes. Remove from the oven and let stand for 10 minutes before cutting.

SERVES 6

Bandiera means "flag," and this lasagne is so named because its components are red, white, and green—the colors of the Italian flag. If you use bottled pasta sauce and no-boil lasagna noodles, it will cut the preparation time in half.

Pesto Lasagne Bandiera

FOR THE PESTO

2 garlic cloves

1/4 cup pine nuts

1 1/2 cups fresh basil leaves, packed

1/4 teaspoon salt

Freshly ground black pepper to taste

1/3 cup extra virgin olive oil

1/4 cup freshly grated Parmesan or soy Parmesan cheese

FOR THE LASAGNE

1 pound lasagna noodles

1 pound firm tofu, drained and blotted dry

12 ounces soft or silken tofu

1 cup pesto

Salt and freshly ground black pepper to taste

3 cups tomato-based pasta sauce, store-bought or homemade

1 cup shredded mozzarella or soy mozzarella cheese

2 tablespoons minced fresh Italian parsley, for garnish

1 To make the pesto, place the garlic and pine nuts in a food processor and pulse until coarsely chopped. Add the basil leaves, salt, and pepper and blend thoroughly to a paste, scraping down the sides of the bowl as necessary. With the machine running, slowly pour the olive oil through the feed tube and process until well blended. Transfer to a small bowl and stir in the Parmesan.

2 To prepare the lasagna, cook the lasagna noodles according to the package directions. Preheat the oven to 350°F.

3 Crumble the firm tofu into a large bowl. Add the soft tofu and pesto, and mix until well combined. Season with salt and pepper. Spoon a layer of the pasta sauce into the bottom of a 9 x 13-inch baking dish. Top with a layer of noodles. Spread half of the tofu mixture evenly over the noodles. Repeat with another layer of noodles, sauce, and the remaining tofu mixture. Finish with a final layer of noodles and sauce, and top with the mozzarella cheese. Cover with foil and bake for 35 minutes. Uncover and bake for 10 minutes longer. Remove from the oven and let stand for 10 minutes before cutting. Garnish with parsley and serve.

SERVES 6

Wild mushrooms, butternut squash, and pecans make this out-of-the-ordinary lasagne extraordinary. Serve with steamed broccoli or another green vegetable.

Autumn Harvest Lasagne

1 tablespoon extra virgin olive oil

1 medium-size onion, minced

1 pound butternut squash, peeled and coarsely grated

1 garlic clove, minced

8 ounces porcini mushrooms, sliced (about 2 cups)

1 teaspoon dried thyme

Salt and freshly ground black pepper to taste

1 pound lasagna noodles

1 pound soft tofu

1 cup milk or soy milk

$1/2$ cup chopped pecans, toasted

$1/4$ cup minced fresh Italian parsley

1 cup shredded mozzarella or soy mozzarella cheese

1 Heat the oil in a saucepan over medium heat. Add the onion, squash, and garlic and cover and cook for 10 minutes, or until soft. Add the mushrooms, thyme, and salt and pepper. Cook for 5 minutes. Transfer to a bowl and set aside.

2 Preheat the oven to 375°F. Cook the lasagna noodles according to the package directions.

3 Combine the tofu, milk, and salt to taste in a food processor and process until well blended. Spread a thin layer of the tofu mixture in the bottom of a 9 x 13-inch baking dish. Arrange a layer of the noodles on top of the tofu mixture, and top with half of the squash mixture. Sprinkle with half of the pecans and half of the parsley. Top with layers of the remaining tofu, noodles, and squash. Top with the cheese and the remaining pecans and parsley, and bake for 45 minutes. Remove from the oven and let stand for 10 minutes before cutting.

SERVES 6

I think this vegetarian version is as rich and satisfying as the original Greek lamb-based dish. It's an ideal party food because you can assemble it ahead and bake it just before serving. To further the no-fuss theme, I serve it with marinated green beans and cherry tomatoes with toasted pine nuts, which I also prepare in advance.

Vegetable Pastitsio

12 ounces elbow macaroni

1 tablespoon extra virgin olive oil

1 medium-size onion, chopped

2 garlic cloves, chopped

One 12-ounce package frozen vegetarian burger crumbles

1/2 teaspoon dried oregano

1/2 teaspoon ground cinnamon

1/4 cup dry red wine

2 cups tomato-based pasta sauce, store-bought or homemade

1/4 cup chopped fresh Italian parsley

3/4 cup soft tofu

2 cups milk or soy milk

1/2 teaspoon salt

1/8 teaspoon freshly ground black pepper

Pinch of nutmeg

1/2 cup freshly grated Parmesan or soy Parmesan cheese

1   Cook the macaroni in a large pot of salted boiling water, stirring occasionally, until it is *al dente*. Drain and set aside.

2   Heat the oil in a large skillet over medium heat. Add the onion and cook until softened, about 5 minutes. Stir in the garlic, burger crumbles, oregano, cinnamon, and wine and simmer to cook off some of the alcohol. Stir in the pasta sauce and parsley and cook over low heat for 10 minutes to blend the flavors.

3   While the sauce is cooking, combine the tofu, milk, salt, pepper, and nutmeg in a blender or food processor, and blend until well combined.

4   Preheat the oven to 375°F. Lightly oil a 9 x 13-inch baking dish.

5   Spread half of the macaroni in the prepared dish and sprinkle with half of the cheese. Spread all of the tomato sauce over the top and layer the remaining macaroni over the tomato sauce. Spread the tofu mixture over the top and sprinkle with the remaining cheese. Bake for 40 minutes or until bubbly and lightly browned on top. Let stand at room temperature for 10 minutes before cutting into squares to serve.

SERVES 6

Use lasagna noodles to create pasta spirals for a lovely presentation. I like to serve them with roasted pencil-thin asparagus and a wedge of warm focaccia bread. A light fruity Barolo is a good wine choice.

Tomato-Basil Pasta Spirals

2 tablespoons extra virgin olive oil

4 shallots, minced

2 tablespoons tomato paste

1/4 cup dry red wine

One 16-ounce can plum tomatoes, drained and finely chopped

Salt and freshly ground black pepper to taste

1/4 cup minced fresh basil

12 lasagna noodles

1 garlic clove, minced

1 pound firm tofu, drained, blotted dry, and crumbled

3 oil-packed sun-dried tomatoes, chopped

1/4 cup pesto, store-bought or homemade (page 71)

1/3 cup fresh bread crumbs

1 teaspoon salt

1/8 teaspoon cayenne pepper

Whole basil leaves, for garnish

1 Heat 1 tablespoon of the oil in a saucepan over medium-low heat. Add half of the shallots and cook for 5 minutes, stirring frequently. Stir in the tomato paste, then add the wine, tomatoes, and salt and pepper. Simmer for 10 minutes, stir in the minced basil, and keep warm over low heat.

2 Cook the noodles in a large pot of salted boiling water, stirring occasionally, until they are *al dente*. Drain, lay them flat on a work surface, and pat dry.

3 Heat the remaining oil in a small skillet over medium heat, add the remaining shallots and the garlic, and cook until soft, about 5 minutes. Transfer the mixture to a food processor and add the tofu, sun-dried tomatoes, pesto, bread crumbs, salt, and cayenne. Process until well blended. Transfer the mixture to a bowl and refrigerate for 30 minutes.

4   Preheat the oven to 350°F. Lightly oil a shallow 9 x 13-inch baking pan.

5   Divide the filling equally among the noodles, spreading it onto the surface of each noodle. Roll up each noodle tightly into a spiral-shaped roll. Place the pasta spirals seam-side down on the prepared pan. Lightly nap the spirals with 1 cup of the sauce. Cover the pan with foil and bake for 20 minutes or until hot.

6   Spread a small amount of sauce on each plate, remove the spirals from the pan, and stand them upright on top of the sauce. Spoon the remaining sauce over the pasta spirals and garnish with whole basil leaves.

SERVES 4

Similar to macaroni and cheese, this family favorite has a taste of the Southwest thanks to picante sauce, chiles, and other spicy ingredients. A green salad would make a nice addition to the meal.

Southwestern Pasta Gratin

8 ounces elbow macaroni

1 tablespoon extra virgin olive oil

2 garlic cloves, minced

1 jalapeño chile, seeded and minced

1½ cups cooked or canned pinto beans, rinsed and drained if canned

1 tablespoon chili powder, or more to your taste

½ teaspoon dried oregano

1½ cups picante sauce, store-bought or homemade

One 14.5-ounce can diced tomatoes, drained

Salt and freshly ground black pepper to taste

1 cup shredded cheddar or soy cheddar cheese

1 Cook the macaroni in a large pot of salted boiling water, stirring occasionally, until it is *al dente*. Drain and set aside.

2 Preheat the oven to 350°F. Lightly oil a 2½-quart baking dish.

3 Heat the oil in a large skillet over low heat, add the garlic and jalapeño, and cook until softened, about 1 minute. Add the beans, chili powder, and oregano. Stir in the picante sauce and tomatoes and mix well. Reduce the heat to low and simmer for 5 minutes. Season with salt and pepper.

4 In a large bowl, combine the macaroni with the bean and tomato mixture and transfer to the prepared dish. Top with the cheese. Cover and bake for 25 minutes. Uncover and continue baking 5 to 10 minutes longer or until the top is lightly browned.

SERVES 4

The ditalini stuffing complements the peppers perfectly and makes a nice change of pace from rice for stuffed pepper enthusiasts. Accompany with a green salad and crusty Italian bread for a satisfying meal.

Pasta-Stuffed Peppers

8 ounces ditalini

6 large green or red bell peppers, tops cut off and seeds removed

2 tablespoons extra virgin olive oil

1 small yellow onion, minced

1 garlic clove, minced

One 16-ounce can plum tomatoes, drained and finely chopped

2 tablespoons raisins

2 tablespoons minced fresh Italian parsley

1 teaspoon minced fresh basil, or 1/2 teaspoon dried

1/8 teaspoon red pepper flakes, or to taste

1/2 teaspoon salt

1/4 teaspoon freshly ground black pepper

1/2 cup dried bread crumbs

1/2 cup freshly grated Parmesan or soy Parmesan cheese

1 Cook the ditalini in a large pot of salted boiling water until it is *al dente*. Drain and set aside.

2 Cook the bell peppers in a large pot of boiling water for 5 minutes to soften them slightly. Drain them and set aside.

3 Heat 1 tablespoon of the oil in large skillet over medium heat. Add the onion and cook until soft, about 5 minutes. Add the garlic, tomatoes, raisins, parsley, basil, red pepper flakes, salt, and pepper. Simmer over low heat for 15 minutes to blend.

4 Combine the cooked ditalini with the tomato sauce in a bowl and mix well. Combine the remaining oil with the bread crumbs and Parmesan in a small bowl. Toss with a fork and set aside.

5 Preheat the oven to 375°F. Lightly oil a 2-quart baking dish and add 1/2 inch of water on the bottom.

6 Stuff the peppers with the pasta mixture, then sprinkle with the crumb mixture and place in the prepared dish. Cover with foil and bake for 30 minutes or until the peppers are tender. Uncover and bake 5 to 10 minutes longer to brown the topping.

SERVES 4 TO 6

Baked Dishes

Swiss chard is a member of the beet family and, despite its name, is native to the regions of the Mediterranean. It is especially high in vitamins A and C, and is rich in iron, calcium, and potassium. If chard is unavailable, spinach may be substituted.

Lemony Chard-Stuffed Shells

12 large pasta shells

2 tablespoons extra virgin olive oil

1/2 cup minced shallots

1 bunch Swiss chard, coarsely chopped

4 ounces white mushrooms, chopped (about 1 cup)

1 pound firm tofu, drained, blotted dry, and crumbled

1/3 cup freshly grated Parmesan or soy Parmesan cheese

Juice and zest of 1 lemon

1/2 teaspoon salt

1/4 teaspoon freshly ground black pepper

3 cups tomato-based pasta sauce, store-bought or homemade

1 Cook the shells in a large pot of salted boiling water, stirring occasionally, until they are *al dente*. Drain and set aside.

2 Heat the oil in a large skillet. Add the shallots and cook until softened, about 5 minutes. Add the chard and mushrooms and cook until just tender, about 5 minutes. Transfer the mixture to a large bowl. Add the tofu, Parmesan, lemon juice and zest, salt, and pepper and mix well.

3 Preheat the oven to 350°F.

4 Using a teaspoon, stuff the filling into the shells until well packed. Spread a layer of the pasta sauce in the bottom of a shallow 9 x 13-inch baking dish. Arrange the shells on top of the sauce, and pour the remaining sauce over and around the shells. Cover and bake for 30 minutes or until hot.

SERVES 4

Based on the early-twentieth-century gratin made with turkey and noodles, this version uses tofu with the requisite sherry and almonds. Although it is named for the famous opera star Luisa Tetrazzini, most authorities agree that it is doubtful that she ever tasted the dish. Steamed green beans, warm dinner rolls, and a fruity white wine round out the meal.

Tetrazzini-Style Fettuccine

12 ounces fettuccine

2 tablespoons extra virgin olive oil

3 to 4 shallots, minced

1 pound firm tofu, drained, blotted dry, and cut into 1/2-inch cubes

8 ounces white mushrooms, sliced (about 2 cups)

1/4 cup dry sherry

1/2 teaspoon salt

1/8 teaspoon freshly ground black pepper

1 cup Vegetable Stock (page 11) or water

1 tablespoon cornstarch dissolved in 2 tablespoons water

1 cup milk or soy milk

3/4 cup slivered toasted almonds

1 cup shredded Monterey Jack or soy mozzarella cheese

1/4 cup dried bread crumbs

1   Cook the fettuccine in a large pot of salted boiling water, stirring occasionally, until it is *al dente*. Drain and set aside.

2   Preheat the oven to 375°F. Lightly oil a 9 x 13-inch baking dish.

3   Heat the oil in a large skillet over medium heat. Add the shallots and cook until soft, about 5 minutes. Add the tofu and mushrooms and cook for 5 minutes, or until the tofu is lightly browned and the mushrooms are softened. Add the sherry and season with salt and pepper, stirring for 1 minute. Remove from the heat and set aside.

4   In a medium-size saucepan, heat the stock to a boil, whisk in the cornstarch mixture, stirring to thicken, then reduce the heat to low. Slowly stir in the milk and set aside.

5   Combine the cooked pasta, the tofu mixture, the almonds, and half of the cheese in a large bowl. Stir in the sauce and mix well. Transfer the mixture to the prepared dish. Sprinkle the top with the remaining cheese and the bread crumbs. Bake for 30 minutes or until hot.

SERVES 4

The polenta may be made a few days ahead and refrigerated until needed. Then simply cut it into serving-size portions and finish in the oven. If you prefer, you may pan-fry the polenta in a little olive oil instead of baking it.

Baked Polenta with Red Beans and Fresh Tomato Salsa

3¹/₂ cups water

1 teaspoon salt, plus more for seasoning

1 cup medium-grind yellow cornmeal

2 tablespoons minced fresh cilantro leaves

3 tablespoons extra virgin olive oil

Freshly ground black pepper to taste

4 scallions, chopped

1¹/₂ cups cooked or one 15-ounce can dark red kidney or other red beans, rinsed and drained if canned

1 cup Fresh Tomato Salsa (recipe follows), for serving

1   Bring the water to a boil in a large saucepan over high heat. Reduce the heat to medium, add the salt, and slowly whisk in the cornmeal, stirring constantly. Reduce the heat to low and continue to cook, stirring frequently, until thick, 30 to 40 minutes. Stir in 1 tablespoon of the cilantro and 1 tablespoon of the oil and season with salt and pepper to taste.

2   Spoon the polenta into a lightly oiled, shallow 10-inch square baking dish and spread it evenly over the bottom. Refrigerate until firm, at least 30 minutes.

3   Heat 1 tablespoon of the oil in a medium-size skillet over medium heat. Add the scallions and cook until slightly softened, about 1 minute. Stir in the beans, the remaining 1 tablespoon cilantro, and the salsa. Season with salt and pepper to taste. Simmer until the mixture is hot and the flavors are blended, about 5 minutes. Keep warm over very low heat.

4   Preheat the oven to 375°F. Cut the polenta into 4 squares, remove from baking dish, and place on a lightly oiled baking sheet. Brush the tops with the remaining 1 tablespoon of oil and bake until hot and golden brown, about 20 minutes.

5   To serve, transfer the polenta to individual plates, spoon some of the salsa on top, and serve hot.

SERVES 4

This is an easy salsa to make when ripe tomatoes are plentiful. Omit the chile if you prefer a mild salsa, or add a second one if you like it extra hot.

FRESH TOMATO SALSA

3 large ripe tomatoes, peeled, seeded, and chopped

1 hot red chile, seeded and minced

4 scallions, minced

1 garlic clove, finely minced

1 tablespoon fresh lime juice

1/4 cup minced fresh cilantro leaves

Salt and freshly ground black pepper to taste

Combine the tomatoes, chile, scallions, and garlic in a large bowl. Add the lime juice, cilantro, and salt and pepper and stir to combine. Cover and let stand at room temperature for 1 hour before serving. If not using right away, refrigerate for up to 2 days, but bring back to room temperature before serving.

MAKES ABOUT 2 1/2 CUPS

This adaptation of a French country classic features white beans, an important component of the original made with meat. You can use dried beans in this recipe, if you like, but it will take several hours to make, not counting soaking time. By using canned beans, the cassoulet can be ready within an hour from start to finish.

White Bean Cassoulet

2 tablespoons extra virgin olive oil

1 large red onion, chopped

2 medium-size carrots, thinly sliced

2 small parsnips, peeled and chopped

3 garlic cloves, minced

2 teaspoons Dijon mustard

1 tablespoon mellow white miso paste dissolved in 2 tablespoons hot (not boiling) water

1/2 teaspoon dried marjoram

1/2 teaspoon dried thyme

1 large bay leaf

Salt and freshly ground black pepper to taste

3 cups cooked or two 15-ounce cans Great Northern, navy, or other white beans, rinsed and drained if canned

One 14.5-ounce can diced tomatoes, drained and chopped

2 cups Vegetable Stock (page 11) or water, or more as needed

1/2 cup dry toasted bread crumbs

2 tablespoons chopped fresh Italian parsley leaves

1 Preheat the oven to 350°F. Heat the oil in a large skillet over medium heat. Add the onion, carrots, and parsnips. Cover and cook until slightly softened, about 5 minutes. Stir in the garlic and cook, stirring, until fragrant, about 30 seconds.

2 Blend the mustard into the miso mixture and stir it into the vegetables. Add the marjoram, thyme, bay leaf, and salt and pepper and set aside.

3 Place the beans and tomatoes in a lightly oiled casserole dish. Add the vegetable mixture and enough stock just to cover the ingredients, stirring to combine.

4 Cover and bake until the vegetables are tender, about 45 minutes. Remove and discard the bay leaf. Sprinkle with the bread crumbs and parsley and serve hot.

SERVES 4

This traditional Greek casserole made with eggplant lends itself well to a vegetarian interpretation.

Tempeh and Eggplant Moussaka

1 medium-size eggplant, peeled

1 tablespoon extra virgin olive oil

One 8-ounce package tempeh, poached (page 8) and chopped

1 large yellow onion, chopped

2 garlic cloves, minced

1 tablespoon minced fresh oregano leaves or 1 teaspoon dried

1/4 teaspoon ground cinnamon

1/4 teaspoon ground nutmeg

1 cup marinara sauce, store-bought or homemade

Salt and freshly ground black pepper to taste

8 ounces soft silken tofu, drained

1 cup milk or soy milk

1 tablespoon fresh lemon juice

3/4 cup dry bread crumbs

1/2 cup freshly grated Parmesan or soy Parmesan cheese

1 Preheat the oven to 375°F. Cut the eggplant into 1/4-inch-thick slices and place on a lightly oiled baking sheet. Bake until softened, about 20 minutes, turning once. Set aside.

2 Heat the oil in a large skillet over medium heat. Add the tempeh and cook until golden brown, about 5 minutes. Remove with a slotted spoon and set aside.

3 To the same skillet, add the onion, cover, and cook until softened, about 5 minutes. Add the garlic, oregano, cinnamon, and nutmeg and stir until fragrant, about 1 minute. Add the reserved tempeh, the marinara sauce, and salt and pepper. Simmer for 10 minutes to blend the flavors. Set aside.

4 In a blender or food processor, combine the tofu, milk, lemon juice, and salt and pepper to taste. Process until smooth and set aside.

5 Sprinkle a small amount of the bread crumbs evenly over the bottom of a lightly oiled 9 x 13-inch baking dish. Arrange a layer of eggplant over the crumbs, then top with half of the tempeh mixture. Add another layer of eggplant, followed by the remaining tempeh mixture and the remaining eggplant. Pour the sauce evenly over the top and sprinkle with the remaining bread crumbs and the cheese.

6 Bake until hot, about 45 minutes. Let rest for at least 15 minutes before serving.

SERVES 4

To get the most juice from a fresh pomegranate, bring it to room temperature and roll it back and forth between a flat work surface and the palm of your hand. You can also buy bottled pomegranate juice, now available in most supermarkets. Note: This dish may be prepared ahead of time, with the final baking just before you're ready to serve it.

Turkish-Style Stuffed Eggplant with Walnut Sauce

2 medium-size eggplants, halved lengthwise

3 tablespoons extra virgin olive oil

1 large yellow onion, chopped

1/2 teaspoon ground turmeric

1 cup ground walnuts

1 cup Vegetable Stock (page 11) or water

Salt and freshly ground black pepper to taste

2 tablespoons tomato paste

1/4 cup firmly packed light brown sugar or natural sweetener

1/4 cup fresh or store-bought pomegranate juice

2 tablespoons fresh lemon juice

1 small green bell pepper, seeded and chopped

1 cup cooked basmati rice

2 tablespoons minced fresh mint leaves

2 tablespoons minced fresh Italian parsley leaves

1   Preheat the oven to 400°F. Place the eggplant halves cut side down on a lightly oiled baking sheet and bake until partially softened, about 15 minutes. Remove from the oven and set aside to cool.

2   When cool enough to handle, scoop out the inside of the eggplants, leaving 1/4-inch-thick shells intact. Coarsely chop the eggplant flesh and set aside along with the shells.

3   Heat 1 tablespoon of the oil in a medium-size saucepan over medium heat. Add half of the onion, cover, and cook until softened, about 5 minutes. Add the turmeric, 1/2 cup of the walnuts, the stock, and salt and pepper. Bring to a boil, then reduce the heat to medium-low and simmer, stirring occasionally, until the sauce begins to thicken, about 15 minutes.

4   In a small bowl, combine the tomato paste, brown sugar, pomegranate juice, and lemon juice and blend well. Add to the sauce, reduce the heat to low, and simmer while you prepare the rest of the dish.

5   Heat the remaining 2 tablespoons of oil in a large skillet over medium heat. Add the remaining onion and the bell pepper, cover, and cook until softened, about 5 minutes. Stir in the chopped eggplant and salt and pepper to taste. Continue cooking to blend the flavors, about 5 minutes, then transfer the eggplant mixture to a large bowl and stir in the rice, the remaining $^1\!/_2$ cup walnuts, the mint, and parsley. Season with salt and pepper to taste.

6   Divide the stuffing among the eggplant shells and arrange them in a lightly oiled baking dish. Bake until the shells are tender and the filling is hot, about 20 minutes. Serve topped with the walnut sauce.

SERVES 4

SAUCY

PASTAS

Smoky sun-dried tomatoes add a depth of flavor to the fresh-tasting plum tomatoes and basil. This pesto can also be used to make a delicious stuffing for baked stuffed mushrooms. Simply combine the pesto with chopped mushroom stems and bread crumbs, stuff into the mushroom caps, and bake until done.

Spaghettini with Tomato Pesto

4 garlic cloves, chopped

1/4 cup pine nuts

1/2 teaspoon salt

6 fresh ripe plum tomatoes, coarsely chopped

1/2 cup oil-packed sun-dried tomatoes, chopped

1/4 cup chopped fresh basil

1/3 cup extra virgin olive oil

1 pound spaghettini

1   Place the garlic, pine nuts, and salt in a food processor and blend thoroughly to a paste, scraping down the sides of the bowl as necessary. Add the fresh and sun-dried tomatoes and half the basil, and process until well blended. With the machine running, slowly pour the oil through the feed tube and process until blended. Set aside.

2   Cook the spaghettini in a large pot of salted boiling water, stirring occasionally, until it is *al dente*. Drain and place it in a large serving bowl. Add the pesto and toss gently to combine. Sprinkle with the remaining basil and serve immediately.

SERVES 4

The sweet taste of red bell peppers combines with walnuts and garlic for a rich yet fresh-tasting pesto that can also be used as a colorful spread for crostini or a flavorful dip for vegetables.

Ziti with Red Pepper–Walnut Pesto

1 cup walnut pieces, lightly toasted

1 large red bell pepper, coarsely chopped

2 garlic cloves

1/4 cup chopped fresh Italian parsley

1/2 teaspoon salt

1/8 teaspoon freshly ground black pepper

1/3 cup extra virgin olive oil

1 pound ziti

Freshly grated Parmesan or soy Parmesan cheese, for serving

1 Place the walnuts, bell pepper, garlic, parsley, salt, and pepper in a food processor and process until finely chopped. With the machine running, slowly pour the olive oil through the feed tube and process until blended. Set aside.

2 Cook the ziti in a large pot of salted boiling water, stirring occasionally, until it is *al dente*. Drain and place it in a shallow serving bowl. Add the pesto and some grated cheese to taste, and toss well. Serve immediately, with additional grated cheese to pass at the table.

SERVES 4

Although tradition dictates that pesto be served with linguine or other flat-strand pasta, the delicate sweetness of almonds and tarragon in this nontraditional pesto reminds me of springtime, so I like to pair it with farfalle, the whimsical "butterfly" pasta, to complete the mood. For an extra touch of spring, add some lightly steamed tender asparagus or early peas.

Farfalle with Almond-Tarragon Pesto

1/2 cup whole almonds

2 large garlic cloves

3/4 teaspoon salt

1 1/2 cups fresh tarragon leaves

Pinch of cayenne pepper

1/2 cup extra virgin olive oil

1 pound farfalle

1   Place the almonds, garlic, and salt in a food processor and pulse until finely ground, about 45 seconds. Add the tarragon and cayenne and blend thoroughly to a paste, scraping down the sides of the bowl as necessary. With the machine running, slowly pour the olive oil through the feed tube and process until well blended. Set aside.

2   Cook the farfalle in a large pot of salted boiling water, stirring occasionally, until it is *al dente*. Drain and place it in a serving bowl. Add the pesto and toss well. Serve immediately.

SERVES 4

Angel hair pasta, or capelli d'angelo, is a very fine spaghetti that is also called capellini. Protein-rich walnuts also contain iron and magnesium, as well as vitamins A, B, and E. Walnuts are a common ingredient in the cuisine of the Italian region of Liguria.

Angel Hair Pasta with Parsley-Walnut Pesto

2 packed cups fresh Italian parsley

3/4 cup walnut pieces

1 large garlic clove, chopped

1/2 teaspoon salt

Freshly ground black pepper to taste

1/4 cup soft or silken tofu

1/3 cup extra virgin olive oil

1 pound angel hair pasta

1   Place the parsley, walnuts, garlic, salt, and pepper in a food processor and pulse until coarsely ground. Add the tofu and process until smooth. With the machine running, slowly pour the olive oil through the feed tube and process until well blended. Set aside.

2   Cook the angel hair in a large pot of salted boiling water, stirring occasionally, until it is *al dente*. Drain and place it in a serving bowl. Add the pesto and toss well. Serve immediately.

SERVES 4

In my family, red pasta sauce was referred to as "gravy." Like my mother's smooth, rich sauce, this recipe calls for a high-quality tomato paste that is "fried" to mellow out the flavor.

Spaghetti with Red Gravy

1 tablespoon extra virgin olive oil

1 medium-size onion, halved

1 large garlic clove, crushed

One 6-ounce can tomato paste

$1/2$ teaspoon dried oregano

$1^1/2$ cups hot water

One 15-ounce can tomato puree

$1/4$ cup dry red wine

1 bay leaf

Salt and freshly ground black pepper to taste

1 pound spaghetti

Freshly grated Pecorino Romano or soy Parmesan cheese

1 Heat the oil in a large saucepan over medium heat. Add the onion and garlic and cook until fragrant, about 1 minute, being careful not to burn the garlic. Add the tomato paste and oregano and cook, stirring, for 1 minute to heat through. Stir in the water, blending until smooth. Add the tomato puree, wine, and bay leaf and bring to a boil. Reduce the heat to low, season with salt and pepper, and simmer for about 30 minutes or until the sauce thickens. Taste to adjust the seasonings, and remove the onion, garlic, and bay leaf before serving.

2 Cook the spaghetti in a large pot of salted boiling water, stirring occasionally, until it is *al dente*. Drain and place it in a large shallow serving bowl or individual plates. Ladle the sauce over the pasta, sprinkle with grated cheese, and serve, passing a bowl of grated cheese at the table.

SERVES 4

Look for ziti rigate, or ridged ziti—the chunky sauce will adhere better than it will to the smooth variety. The addition of eggplant adds hearty texture to the rich sauce and makes it distinctly Sicilian.

Ziti with Sicilian-Style Tomato Sauce

2 tablespoons extra virgin olive oil

1 small eggplant, cut into 1/2-inch dice

1 small red bell pepper, cut into 1/2-inch dice

1 large garlic clove, crushed

2 tablespoons tomato paste

One 28-ounce can diced tomatoes, drained

1 tablespoon capers, drained

Salt and freshly ground black pepper to taste

1/4 cup chopped fresh basil or 2 teaspoons dried

1 pound ziti

Freshly grated Pecorino Romano or soy Parmesan cheese

1   Heat the oil in a large skillet over medium heat. Add the eggplant and cook, stirring occasionally, until lightly browned, about 10 minutes. Add the bell pepper and garlic and cook until softened, about 5 minutes. Stir in the tomato paste, tomatoes, capers, and salt and pepper to taste and bring to a boil. Reduce the heat to low and simmer for 15 minutes to reduce slightly and blend the flavors. Add the basil and keep warm over low heat.

2   Cook the ziti in a large pot of salted boiling water, stirring occasionally, until it is *al dente*. Drain and place it in a shallow serving bowl. Add the sauce, sprinkle with grated cheese, and toss gently. Serve immediately, passing additional grated cheese at the table.

SERVES 4

This sauce is best made with very ripe tomatoes that are com-
plemented by the faintly licorice flavor of fresh fennel, a popular
vegetable in Italian cooking. When eaten raw, fennel is said to aid
digestion. If you want to make this sauce when tomatoes are out
of season, substitute high-quality canned tomatoes. San Marzano
tomatoes, imported from Italy, are especially good.

Fresh Tomato and Fennel Sauce over Linguine

2 pounds ripe tomatoes

2 tablespoons extra virgin olive oil

1 medium-size yellow onion, minced

1 fennel bulb, thinly sliced

1 large garlic clove, minced

2 tablespoons tomato paste

1/2 cup Vegetable Stock (page 11) or water

1 tablespoon chopped fresh basil or
    1 teaspoon dried

1 teaspoon minced fresh oregano or
    1/4 teaspoon dried

1 teaspoon salt

Freshly ground black pepper to taste

1 pound linguine

Freshly grated Parmesan or soy Parmesan
    cheese, for serving

1   Cut an "x" on the bottom of each tomato with a sharp knife and plunge them into boiling water for 30 seconds. Remove from the water and peel off the skins. Coarsely chop
the tomatoes and set aside.

2   Heat the oil in a large saucepan over medium heat. Add the onion, fennel, and garlic.
Cover and cook, stirring occasionally, until soft, about 5 minutes. Uncover, stir in the
tomato paste, tomatoes, and stock, and bring to a boil. If using dried herbs, add them
now. Reduce heat to low, add the salt and pepper and simmer for about 30 minutes or
until a thick, rich consistency is reached. If using fresh basil and oregano, stir in at
this time. Adjust the seasonings to taste and keep warm over low heat.

3   Cook the linguine in a large pot of salted boiling water, stirring occasionally, until it
is *al dente*. Drain and place it in a large shallow serving bowl or individual plates.
Ladle the sauce over the pasta and serve with grated cheese.

SERVES 4

Tofu provides added protein along with a creamy texture in this rich-tasting sauce. Good-quality canned tomatoes are imperative to the success of this sauce—imported Italian brands tend to be more flavorful.

Fettuccine with Creamy Tomato Sauce

1 tablespoon extra virgin olive oil

1 small yellow onion, minced

1 garlic clove, crushed

One 28-ounce can diced tomatoes, drained

1 teaspoon dried basil

1/2 teaspoon dried marjoram

Salt and freshly ground black pepper to taste

1/4 cup soft or silken tofu

1 pound fettuccine

2 tablespoons minced fresh Italian parsley

1   Heat the oil in a large saucepan over medium heat. Add the onion, cover, and cook until soft, about 5 minutes. Stir in the garlic, tomatoes, basil, marjoram, and salt and pepper. Simmer the sauce for 20 minutes, stirring occasionally, to blend the flavors and reduce slightly.

2   Place the tofu in a blender or food processor with the sauce and process until smooth. Return to the saucepan and adjust the seasonings to taste. Keep the sauce warm over low heat.

3   Cook the fettuccine in a large pot of salted boiling water, stirring occasionally, until it is *al dente*. Drain and place it in a large serving bowl. Add the sauce and toss to combine. Sprinkle with the parsley and serve immediately.

SERVES 4

For a deeper, more woodsy flavor, eliminate the white mushrooms and use all porcini instead. As another alternative, use one ounce of dried porcini for an even more intense flavor. Reconstitute dried porcini in warm water for 20 minutes before using in the recipe.

Fusilli with Tomato-Mushroom Sauce

2 tablespoons extra virgin olive oil

2 large garlic cloves, minced

4 ounces porcini mushrooms, chopped (about 1 cup)

4 ounces white mushrooms, chopped (about 1 cup)

One 28-ounce can plum tomatoes, drained and chopped

1 teaspoon dried marjoram

Salt and freshly ground black pepper to taste

1 pound fusilli

1   Heat the oil in a large skillet over medium heat. Add the garlic and both kinds of mushrooms, and cook until the vegetables soften, about 5 minutes. Add the tomatoes, marjoram, and salt and pepper. Simmer for 15 minutes to blend the flavors.

2   Cook the fusilli in salted boiling water, stirring occasionally, until it is *al dente*. Drain and place it in a large serving bowl. Add the sauce, and toss gently to combine.

SERVES 4

Explanations for the name vary: Some say this "streetwalker-style" pasta dish is so named because the sauce is too good to resist. Another story relates that it was a quick meal that the ladies of the evening could easily prepare from pantry ingredients after a hard night's work. No cheese is necessary with this extraordinarily flavorful sauce.

Pasta Puttanesca

2 tablespoons extra virgin olive oil

3 large garlic cloves, finely chopped

1/2 teaspoon red pepper flakes, or to taste

2 tablespoons tomato paste

One 28-ounce can diced tomatoes, drained

1 cup pitted black gaeta olives, halved

2 tablespoons capers, drained

1 teaspoon dried basil

Salt and freshly ground black pepper to taste

1 pound spaghetti

2 tablespoons minced fresh Italian parsley

1 Heat the oil in a large saucepan over medium heat. Add the garlic and red pepper flakes and cook until fragrant, about 30 seconds. Stir in the tomato paste, tomatoes, olives, capers, and basil. Season with salt and pepper. Bring the sauce to a boil, then reduce the heat to low and simmer for 10 minutes, stirring occasionally.

2 Cook the spaghetti in a large pot of salted boiling water, stirring occasionally, until it is *al dente*. Drain and place it in a large serving bowl. Add the sauce and toss gently to combine. Sprinkle with the minced parsley and serve immediately.

SERVES 4

There are a variety of vegetarian sausages on the market; however, most are not very spicy and need a little encouragement from your spice cupboard. If veggie sausage is unavailable, use ground veggie burgers or another ground meat alternative and increase the spices to give it a "sausage" flavor.

Cavatelli with Spicy Veggie Sausage and Tomatoes

1 tablespoon extra virgin olive oil

1 carrot, finely chopped

1 medium-size onion, finely chopped

1 garlic clove, minced

2 tablespoons tomato paste

1 tablespoon minced fresh marjoram or 1 teaspoon dried

1 teaspoon ground fennel

One 28-ounce can Italian plum tomatoes, drained and chopped

$^1/_2$ teaspoon salt

$^1/_8$ teaspoon freshly ground black pepper

$^1/_8$ teaspoon cayenne pepper, or to taste

8 ounces frozen vegetarian sausage links or patties, cooked and crumbled

Red pepper flakes to taste

1 pound cavatelli

Freshly shaved Parmesan or grated soy Parmesan cheese, for garnish

Minced fresh Italian parsley, for garnish

1   In a large saucepan, heat the oil over medium heat. Add the carrot, onion, and garlic and cook until soft, 5 to 7 minutes. Stir in the tomato paste, marjoram, ground fennel, and tomatoes. Season with the salt, pepper, and cayenne and simmer for about 20 minutes. Stir in the vegetarian sausage and red pepper flakes to taste, and simmer 5 minutes longer to blend the flavors. Keep warm over low heat.

2   Cook the cavatelli in a large pot of salted boiling water, stirring occasionally, until it is *al dente*. Drain and divide it among individual plates or shallow bowls. Top with the sauce, a few shavings of Parmesan, and a sprinkling of parsley. Serve immediately, passing additional cheese at the table.

SERVES 4

This vivid orange sauce is especially fun at Halloween, when you might consider a strikingly festive garnish of chopped black olives. Canned pumpkin cuts down on preparation time, but fresh pumpkin or winter squash may be used instead.

Rotelle with Spicy Pumpkin Sauce

1 tablespoon extra virgin olive oil

1 small yellow onion, minced

1 small red bell pepper, chopped

1 garlic clove, minced

One 15-ounce can pumpkin puree

1/2 cup Vegetable Stock (page 11) or water

1 tablespoon cornstarch

1 teaspoon salt

1/4 teaspoon allspice

1/8 teaspoon cayenne pepper, or to taste

1/2 cup milk or soy milk

1 pound rotelle

1   Heat the oil in a large skillet over medium heat. Add the onion, bell pepper, and garlic, cover, and cook for 10 minutes or until soft. Transfer the vegetable mixture to a food processor and puree. Add the pumpkin, stock, cornstarch, salt, allspice, and cayenne and process until smooth. Transfer to a saucepan, stir in the milk, and heat to a simmer, stirring constantly for 8 to 10 minutes to thicken and heat through. Adjust the seasonings to taste, and keep warm over very low heat.

2   Cook the rotelle in a large pot of salted boiling water, stirring occasionally, until it is *al dente*. Drain and place it in a shallow serving bowl. Spoon the sauce over the pasta, and serve immediately.

SERVES 4

2/14 Made w/ Chicken broth & almond milk
Not bad but very bland. Next time consider
not pureeing it.

Bottled green peppercorns packed in brine are available in specialty food stores and well-stocked supermarkets. They have a piquant bite, so alter the amount used according to your taste. Mild white mushrooms are preferred in this dish because the flavor of more assertive wild mushrooms would compete with the flavor of the peppercorns.

Fettuccine with Creamy Mushroom and Green Peppercorn Sauce

2 tablespoons extra virgin olive oil

3 shallots, chopped

8 ounces white mushrooms, sliced (about 2 cups)

2 tablespoons all-purpose flour

2 cups milk or soy milk

1 to 2 teaspoons green peppercorns, drained

Salt to taste

1 pound fettuccine

1   Heat the oil in a large saucepan over medium heat. Add the shallots and cook for 5 minutes or until softened. Add the mushrooms and cook 2 minutes to soften. Sprinkle the flour over the shallots and mushrooms and cook, stirring, for 1 minute to remove the raw taste from the flour. Reduce the heat to low. Slowly add the milk, stirring constantly to thicken. Add the peppercorns and salt and simmer 5 minutes to allow the flavors to blend. Keep warm over very low heat.

2   Cook the fettuccine in a large pot of salted boiling water, stirring occasionally, until it is *al dente*. Drain and place it in a shallow serving bowl. Add the sauce, toss lightly to combine, and serve immediately.

SERVES 4

Pureed fresh vegetables combine to create a velvety sauce that tastes like a rich indulgence. Vary the vegetables according to your preference and their availability.

Linguine with Summer Vegetable Puree

1 tablespoon extra virgin olive oil

1 small onion, chopped

1 small red bell pepper, chopped

2 garlic cloves, chopped

1 zucchini, peeled and chopped

4 ounces white or cremini mushrooms, chopped (about 1 cup)

4 ripe tomatoes, chopped

2 tablespoons tomato paste

Salt and freshly ground black pepper to taste

1 pound linguine

2 tablespoons chopped fresh basil

1   Heat the oil in a large skillet over medium heat. Add the onion, bell pepper, and garlic, and cook for 5 minutes to soften. Add the zucchini, mushrooms, and tomatoes, and cook 10 to 15 minutes longer, or until the vegetables are very soft. Stir in the tomato paste and salt and pepper. Transfer the mixture to a food processor and puree. Strain the sauce into a saucepan through a fine-mesh strainer, and simmer over low heat for 15 minutes to blend the flavors. Keep warm over low heat, adding a little stock or water if the sauce becomes too thick.

2   Cook the linguine in a large pot of salted boiling water, stirring occasionally, until it is *al dente*. Drain and place it in a shallow serving bowl. Add the sauce and toss to combine. Sprinkle with the basil and serve immediately.

SERVES 4

Cannellini beans flavored with sage are a popular Tuscan combination. Here the pair is pureed into a creamy pasta sauce enlivened with a splash of balsamic vinegar, a slightly sweet and syrupy aged vinegar from Modena, Italy.

Fettuccine with Sage-Cannellini Puree

2 tablespoons extra virgin olive oil

1 small onion, minced

1/4 cup fresh sage leaves, minced

1 1/2 cups cooked cannellini beans, rinsed and drained if canned

1 tablespoon balsamic vinegar

1/2 teaspoon salt

Freshly ground black pepper to taste

1/2 cup hot water (plus more as needed)

1 pound fettuccine

Whole fresh sage leaves, for garnish

1 Heat the oil in a large skillet over medium heat. Add the onion and cook, stirring occasionally, until softened, about 5 minutes. Add the sage and cook for 2 minutes. Add the beans, vinegar, salt, and pepper and stir to blend the flavors. Transfer the bean mixture to a food processor or blender and puree with the water. Return the sauce to the pan and keep warm over low heat, adding more water if the mixture gets too thick.

2 Cook the fettuccine in a large pot of salted boiling water, stirring occasionally, until it is *al dente*. Drain and place it in a large shallow serving bowl. Add the sauce and toss to combine. Serve immediately, garnished with the sage leaves.

SERVES 4

When my mom made chicken cacciatore, I'd skip the chicken and enjoy the vegetables and pappardelle that went with it. Here, I've adapted her recipe using tempeh and fettuccine.

Fettuccine Cacciatore

2 tablespoons extra virgin olive oil

8 ounces poached tempeh (page 8), cut into 1-inch pieces

1/2 cup dry white wine

1 celery rib, coarsely chopped

1 carrot, coarsely chopped

1 green bell pepper, coarsely chopped

1 garlic clove, minced

One 28-ounce can diced tomatoes, drained

1 teaspoon minced fresh rosemary or 1/2 teaspoon dried

1 teaspoon minced fresh marjoram or 1/2 teaspoon dried

Salt and freshly ground black pepper to taste

1 pound fettuccine

1 Heat 1 tablespoon of the oil in a skillet over medium heat. Add the tempeh and cook until lightly browned, about 5 minutes. Remove the tempeh from the skillet and set aside. Deglaze the pan with the wine, stirring to scrape up any browned bits. Reduce the wine by half and set aside.

2 Heat the remaining oil in a large saucepan over medium heat. Add the celery, carrot, bell pepper, and garlic. Cover and cook until soft, about 10 minutes. Remove the cover, add the tomatoes, rosemary, and marjoram, and season with salt and pepper. Simmer the sauce for 10 minutes, then add the tempeh and wine, and simmer for 20 minutes longer. Keep warm over low heat.

3 Cook the fettuccine in a large pot of salted boiling water, stirring occasionally, until it is *al dente*. Drain and place it in a serving bowl. Top with the sauce and serve immediately.

SERVES 4

The peppery flavor of the arugula provides the perfect complement to the mellow fava beans. Fresh favas can be difficult to find but well worth it when you do. You will need to peel the tough skin from the favas before cooking, unless you're lucky enough to find the highly prized tender young beans.

Ziti with Arugula and Fava Beans

1 cup peeled fava beans

2 tablespoons extra virgin olive oil

2 garlic cloves, sliced paper thin

1 bunch arugula, stems trimmed

1/2 cup Vegetable Stock (page 11) or water

Salt and freshly ground black pepper to taste

1 pound ziti

1 tablespoon minced fresh Italian parsley

Freshly grated Pecorino Romano or soy Parmesan cheese, for serving

1   Cook the fava beans in boiling water until just tender, 5 to 7 minutes. Drain and set aside.

2   Heat the oil in a large skillet over medium heat. Add the garlic, arugula, and stock and cook, stirring until the arugula is wilted, about 3 minutes. Add the reserved beans, season with salt and pepper, and cook 5 minutes longer. Keep warm over low heat.

3   Cook the ziti in a large pot of salted boiling water, stirring occasionally, until it is *al dente*. Drain and place it in a large serving bowl. Add the arugula-bean mixture and parsley, and toss gently to combine. Serve immediately, passing grated cheese at the table.

SERVES 4

Although lentils are more prominent in Indian and Middle Eastern cooking, they are also used in Italian cuisine. This thin lens-shaped legume is rich in protein, calcium, iron, and B-complex vitamins. Since lentils do not require soaking and cook up quickly, this recipe doesn't require a lot of advance planning to get dinner on the table.

Linguine with Red Lentil Sauce

¾ cup dried red lentils, rinsed and picked over

2 carrots, cut diagonally in ¼-inch slices

1 celery rib, diced

3 tablespoons extra virgin olive oil

1 garlic clove, minced

One 6-ounce can tomato paste

Salt and freshly ground black pepper to taste

1 pound linguine

2 tablespoons chopped fresh Italian parsley

1 Place the lentils, carrots, and celery in a pot of salted boiling water. Reduce the heat to medium-low and simmer until tender, about 30 minutes.

2 Drain the lentils and vegetables, reserving 2 cups of the cooking liquid. Toss the lentil mixture with 1 tablespoon of the oil and set aside.

3 Heat the remaining 2 tablespoons of oil in a large skillet over medium heat. Add the garlic and cook until fragrant, about 30 seconds. Stir in the tomato paste and cook for 2 minutes to mellow the flavor of the paste. Stir in the lentil cooking liquid, blending until smooth. Add the lentil mixture and salt and pepper. Simmer over low heat to blend the flavors. If the liquid evaporates, add some water.

4 Cook the linguine in a large pot of salted boiling water, stirring occasionally, until it is *al dente*. Drain and divide it among individual plates or shallow bowls. Top with the sauce, sprinkle with the parsley, and serve immediately.

SERVES 4

11/11 — good but bland, could guse more salt, pepper & spices esp since haven't been using tomato -- uses pumpkin instead

Peanuts, lime, and chili paste give this dish a Thai flavor. You decide how much or how little chili paste you want to use. Thai beer makes a good accompaniment.

Fettuccine and Green Beans with Peanut Sauce

1/2 cup peanut butter

1 garlic clove, minced

3 tablespoons tamari

2 teaspoons brown sugar

1 tablespoon fresh lime juice

1/2 teaspoon hot chili paste, or to taste

1 1/2 cups Vegetable Stock (page 11) or water

12 ounces fettuccine

12 ounces green beans, ends trimmed and cut into 1-inch pieces (about 3 cups)

2 tablespoons minced fresh cilantro or Thai basil

2 tablespoons chopped roasted peanuts

1   In a food processor or blender, combine the peanut butter, garlic, tamari, brown sugar, lime juice, chili paste, and 1/2 cup of the stock. Blend until smooth. Transfer the peanut sauce to a saucepan and stir in as much of the remaining stock as needed to give it a smooth, saucelike consistency. Heat the sauce over low heat, stirring until it is hot, then keep it warm over very low heat.

2   Cook the fettuccine in a large pot of salted boiling water, stirring occasionally. When the pasta has cooked for about 3 minutes, add the green beans to the cooking pasta. When the pasta is *al dente*, drain the pasta and green beans, and place in a large bowl. Add the peanut sauce and toss to combine. Transfer to individual plates and garnish with cilantro and chopped peanuts. Serve immediately.

SERVES 4

A mild curry paste may be substituted for the hot, if you prefer. Serve with a choice of condiments on the table: Small bowls containing chutney, chopped peanuts, shredded unsweetened coconut, scallions, and raisins can be offered to suit individual preferences.

Creamy Noodle Curry

1 tablespoon safflower oil

1 medium-size onion, chopped

2 garlic cloves, minced

1 1/2 tablespoons hot curry paste, or to taste

One 14.5-ounce can diced tomatoes, undrained

1 1/2 cups cooked or canned chickpeas, rinsed and drained if canned

1/2 cup soft or silken tofu

1 cup low-fat unsweetened coconut milk

Salt and freshly ground black pepper to taste

1 pound fettuccine

8 ounces green beans, ends trimmed and cut into 1-inch pieces (2 cups)

1   Heat the oil in a large skillet over medium heat. Add the onion and cook for 5 minutes to soften. Stir in the garlic and curry paste and cook for 2 minutes, stirring to blend. Stir in the tomatoes and their liquid, and simmer for 5 minutes to blend the flavors. Add the chickpeas and keep warm over low heat.

2   In a food processor or blender, combine the tofu with the coconut milk, and add salt and pepper. Blend until smooth. Stir the tofu mixture into the vegetable mixture and keep warm over low heat.

3   Cook the fettuccine in a large pot of salted boiling water, stirring occasionally. When the pasta has cooked for about 3 minutes, add the green beans. When the pasta is *al dente*, drain the fettuccine and green beans, and place in a large serving bowl. Add the curried vegetables and toss to combine. Serve immediately.

SERVES 4

Olivada, a puree of ripe olives, adds richness to this hearty, zesty, Italian-style sauce. If you want a change of pace from pasta, try serving this over polenta.

Olivada, Tomato, and Chickpea Sauce over Penne

¾ cup ripe black olives, pitted

¼ cup extra virgin olive oil

1 medium-size onion, chopped

1 fennel bulb, chopped

3 garlic cloves, minced

1 small green bell pepper, chopped

2 cups fresh or canned diced tomatoes

One 6-ounce can tomato paste

1 teaspoon paprika

1 teaspoon dried oregano

2 cups water

1 teaspoon salt

¼ teaspoon freshly ground black pepper

½ teaspoon red pepper flakes

1½ cups cooked or canned chickpeas, rinsed and drained if canned

One 12-ounce package frozen vegetarian sausage links or patties, cooked and crumbled

1 pound penne

1   Place the olives in a food processor, and puree. Slowly stream in 3 tablespoons of the oil until well blended. Transfer the olivada to a small bowl, and set aside.

2   Heat the remaining 1 tablespoon oil in a large pot over medium heat. Add the onion, fennel, garlic, and bell pepper, cover, and cook until the vegetables are softened, about 10 minutes. Add the tomatoes, tomato paste, paprika, oregano, water, salt, pepper, red pepper flakes, chickpeas, and vegetarian sausage. Stir well to combine, lower the heat, and simmer, uncovered, for 30 minutes.

3   Cook the penne in a large pot of salted boiling water, stirring occasionally, until *al dente*. Drain and place it in a large bowl. Pour the sauce over the pasta, stir to combine, and ladle into individual bowls, drizzling the olivada over each portion.

SERVES 4

STIR-FRIES

AND

SAUTÉS

Fresh bean sprouts and peanuts add a delightful crunch, and protein, to this quick and easy dish made with fragrant jasmine rice and spicy basil. Thai basil can be found in Asian markets, but if it is unavailable, substitute regular basil. Fresh bean sprouts are also available in Asian markets and in well-stocked supermarkets. Thai bird's eye chiles are super hot; you can substitute a milder variety, or even omit the chile if you prefer.

Thai Fried Rice

1 tablespoon safflower oil

1 small onion, finely chopped

1/2 of a red bell pepper, finely chopped

1/2 cup grated carrots

1 garlic clove, minced

1 teaspoon minced fresh ginger

1 small Thai chile (optional), minced

4 cups cold cooked jasmine rice

2 tablespoons tamari

2 scallions, trimmed and finely minced

2 tablespoons minced fresh Thai basil

1/2 cup fresh bean sprouts

2 tablespoons chopped peanuts

Heat the oil in a large skillet or wok over medium-high heat until hot. Add the onion and stir-fry for 3 to 4 minutes, or until soft. Add the bell pepper, carrots, garlic, ginger, and chile, if using, and stir-fry for 2 minutes, or until slightly softened and fragrant. Add the rice and tamari and stir-fry for 3 minutes, or until the rice is heated through. Stir in the scallions and basil. Serve sprinkled with the bean sprouts and peanuts.

SERVES 4

Vegetarian oyster sauce, also made from soy sauce, can be found in well-stocked Asian markets. If it's unavailable, just omit it—the dish will still be good.

Jasmine Rice with Slivered Tofu

1 pound extra-firm tofu, drained and blotted dry

2 tablespoons tamari

1 tablespoon vegetarian oyster sauce

1 teaspoon light brown sugar

1 tablespoon vegetable oil

2 teaspoons minced garlic

1/2 to 2 Thai chiles, to your taste, thinly sliced

1/2 cup thinly sliced red onion

1 cup chopped fresh Thai basil

4 cups hot cooked jasmine rice

1   Cut the tofu into 1/4-inch-thick slices and place on a baking sheet lined with paper towels to absorb excess liquid. Cover with more paper towels, place another baking sheet on top, and press down to extract excess water. Cut the tofu into matchstick slivers and set aside.

2   Combine the tamari, oyster sauce, and brown sugar in a small bowl. Set aside.

3   Heat the oil in a large skillet or wok over medium-high heat. Add the tofu, in batches if necessary, and cook, stirring until golden, about 30 seconds. Remove and set aside. Add the garlic and stir-fry for 10 seconds, or until fragrant. Add the chiles and onion and stir-fry for 30 seconds, or until softened. Add the tamari mixture, the basil, and the tofu and stir-fry for 1 minute, or until hot. Place the rice in a shallow serving bowl or on individual plates, top with the tofu mixture, and serve.

SERVES 4

Vary the vegetables in this easy stir-fry according to personal preference and the season. To underscore the flavor of the peanut sauce, sprinkle on some chopped peanuts for garnish.

Vegetables and Rice with Thai Peanut Sauce

1 tablespoon safflower oil

1 tablespoon minced garlic

1 small Thai chile (optional), seeded and minced

1/2 cup chopped scallions

1 tablespoon finely chopped fresh ginger

2 tablespoons tamari

1/2 cup water

1 teaspoon sugar

2 cups small cauliflower florets

1 pound green beans, ends trimmed and cut into 2-inch pieces

12 cherry tomatoes, halved

Thai Peanut Sauce (recipe follows)

4 to 5 cups hot cooked jasmine rice

Heat the oil in a large skillet or wok over medium-high heat. Add the garlic, chile, if using, the scallions, and ginger and stir-fry for 1 minute, or until fragrant. Add the tamari, water, sugar, cauliflower, and green beans and stir and combine for 2 minutes, or until the vegetables begin to soften. Reduce the heat, cover, and simmer for 2 minutes longer, or until the vegetables are tender. Uncover, add the cherry tomatoes and peanut sauce, and toss gently to heat through. Serve at once over the hot cooked rice.

SERVES 4

Be forewarned: This peanut sauce is addictive—you'll want to use it on everything. Try it as a dipping sauce for steamed fresh vegetables or spring rolls. For a thinner sauce, blend in a little water.

THAI PEANUT SAUCE

⅓ cup creamy peanut butter

¼ cup unsweetened coconut milk

1 tablespoon fresh lime juice

1 tablespoon tamari

2 teaspoons light brown sugar

1 teaspoon Asian chili paste, or to taste

In a small bowl, whisk together the peanut butter, coconut milk, lime juice, tamari, brown sugar, and chili paste until well blended. Taste to adjust the seasoning. Use at once, or cover and refrigerate until ready to use. This sauce will keep well for up to 1 week. Bring to room temperature before using.

MAKES ABOUT 3/4 CUP

Vietnamese cuisine is similar to Thai with its use of such ingredients as lemongrass and cilantro, but it tends to be sweeter and less spicy. Rice noodles are extremely popular in Vietnam, but the Vietnamese also eat a great deal of jasmine and sticky rice.

Vietnamese-Style Tempeh with Lemongrass and Cilantro

One 2-inch piece lemongrass

1 tablespoon safflower oil

8 ounces poached tempeh (page 8), cut into 1/2-inch cubes

1/2 cup thinly sliced red bell pepper

3 tablespoons tamari

1 tablespoon rice vinegar

1 tablespoon light brown sugar

1 teaspoon Asian chili paste

4 scallions, trimmed and minced

4 to 5 cups hot cooked jasmine rice

3 tablespoons chopped fresh cilantro, for garnish

1   Remove the tough outer layer from the lemongrass and discard. Finely chop the remaining inner section and set aside.

2   Heat the oil in a large skillet or wok over medium-high heat. Add the tempeh and stir-fry until browned, about 4 minutes. Add the bell pepper and lemongrass and stir-fry for 1 minute. Add the tamari, vinegar, brown sugar, chili paste, and scallions and stir to combine. Taste and adjust the seasoning if necessary. Spoon over the hot cooked rice and top with the chopped cilantro.

SERVES 4

Bright green broccoli florets spiced with a garlicky ginger sauce provide a striking contrast to tofu and snowy white rice.

Spicy Tofu and Broccoli Stir-Fry

1/4 cup tamari

2 tablespoons water

1 teaspoon sugar (or a natural sweetener to taste)

1/4 teaspoon salt

1 tablespoon toasted sesame oil

2 teaspoons cornstarch

1 tablespoon safflower oil

4 cups broccoli florets

1 tablespoon minced garlic

1 tablespoon minced fresh ginger

1/2 teaspoon red pepper flakes

8 ounces firm tofu, drained, blotted dry, and cut into 1/2-inch cubes

3 tablespoons minced scallions

4 to 5 cups hot cooked long-grain white rice

1   In a small bowl, stir together the tamari, water, sugar, salt, sesame oil, and corn-starch. Set aside.

2   In a large skillet or wok, heat the safflower oil over medium-high heat until hot. Add the broccoli and stir-fry for 1 minute, or until bright green. With a slotted spoon, transfer to paper towels to drain. Add the garlic, ginger, red pepper flakes, and tofu to the pan and stir-fry for 2 minutes. Return the broccoli to the pan and stir-fry for 1 minute. Add the tamari mixture and the scallions and stir-fry for 1 minute, or until the broccoli is tender and well coated with the sauce. Serve over the rice.

SERVES 4

Hoisin sauce, a flavorful Chinese condiment similar to barbecue sauce, adds an exotic sweet spiciness to any stir-fry. It can be found in Asian markets and well-stocked supermarkets. I like the taste and textural effect achieved by combining half white and half brown rice, but any rice would be great in this recipe.

Hoisin-Glazed Tofu over Rice

1 pound extra-firm tofu, drained and blotted dry

1/4 cup hoisin sauce

2 tablespoons tamari

2 tablespoons water

1 tablespoon safflower oil

1 tablespoon minced fresh ginger

2 tablespoons minced scallions

1/4 teaspoon red pepper flakes

2 1/2 cups cooked long-grain white rice

2 1/2 cups cooked long-grain brown rice

1 tablespoon toasted sesame oil

1   Cut the tofu into 1/2-inch-wide slices and set aside. In a small bowl, combine the hoisin, tamari, and water. Set aside.

2   Heat the safflower oil in a large skillet or wok over medium heat. Add the tofu, ginger, scallions, and red pepper flakes and stir-fry for 3 minutes, or until fragrant. Add the hoisin mixture and bring to a simmer, stirring until heated through, about 5 minutes.

3   Meanwhile, in a large skillet or saucepan, heat both rices together with the sesame oil, tossing to coat. Serve the tofu over the rice.

SERVES 4

Tempeh is made of compressed fermented soybeans, which are formed into cakes, like tofu. Its meaty texture is terrific in stir-fries such as this one, where it stands up well to the assertiveness of the spicy Szechwan seasonings.

Szechwan Tempeh over Rice

1 tablespoon safflower oil

1 pound poached tempeh (page 8), cut into
  1/2-inch-wide slices

1 carrot, cut diagonally into 1/4-inch slices

1 green bell pepper, cut into 1-inch pieces

1 garlic clove, minced

2 teaspoons minced fresh ginger

2 scallions, minced

1/4 teaspoon red pepper flakes

2 tablespoons dry sherry

2 tablespoons tamari

1/2 cup Vegetable Stock (page 11) or water

1 tablespoon cornstarch dissolved in
  2 tablespoons water

4 to 5 cups hot cooked long-grain white or
  brown rice

Heat the oil in a large skillet or wok over medium-high heat. Add the tempeh and stir-fry until golden, about 5 minutes. Add the carrot and bell pepper and stir-fry for 2 minutes, or until slightly softened. Stir in the garlic, ginger, scallions, and red pepper flakes and stir-fry for about 30 seconds, until fragrant. Stir in the sherry, tamari, and stock. Then stir in the cornstarch mixture and cook until the sauce thickens. Serve over the rice.

SERVES 4

Donburi is usually made with eggs, but for a vegetarian version, silken tofu stands in nicely. Serve in oversized rice bowls for an authentic touch. Japanese sticky rice is traditional, but any variety of rice would work well in this dish.

Vegetable Donburi

1 pound firm tofu, drained and blotted dry

1 tablespoon safflower oil

1 large onion, finely chopped

1 carrot, grated

4 ounces shiitake mushrooms, stemmed and thinly sliced (about 1 cup)

1/4 cup tamari

1 teaspoon sugar (or a natural sweetener to taste)

4 cups hot cooked Japanese sticky (glutinous) or other rice

1 teaspoon toasted sesame oil

1 tablespoon toasted sesame seeds, for garnish

Crumble the tofu into a bowl and set aside. Heat the safflower oil in a large skillet or wok over medium-high heat. Add the onion and stir-fry until soft, about 5 minutes. Add the carrot and mushrooms and cook about 1 minute longer, until softened. Stir in the tamari, sugar, and tofu, stirring to combine, and cook until the tofu is heated through. Serve over the hot rice, drizzled with the toasted sesame oil and sprinkled with the sesame seeds.

SERVES 4

Although long-grain white rice would be traditional in this Chinese-inspired dish, you might try jasmine or basmati to complement the sweetness of the orange sauce. Asian chili paste is available in Asian grocery stores and well-stocked supermarkets.

Green Beans and Rice with Sesame-Orange Sauce

¾ cup fresh orange juice

1 tablespoon Asian chili paste, or to taste

1 tablespoon light brown sugar

1 tablespoon tamari

1 tablespoon fresh lemon juice

1 tablespoon toasted sesame oil

2 teaspoons safflower oil

2 garlic cloves, minced

1 pound green beans, ends trimmed and halved diagonally

¼ cup minced onion

½ cup water

1 tablespoon arrowroot or cornstarch dissolved in 2 tablespoons water

4 to 5 cups hot cooked long-grain white rice

1 tablespoon toasted sesame seeds, for garnish

1   In a small bowl, combine the orange juice, chili paste, brown sugar, tamari, lemon juice, and sesame oil. Set aside.

2   Heat the safflower oil in a large skillet or wok over medium heat. Add the garlic, green beans, and onion and stir-fry for 2 minutes, then add the water, cover, and steam until the vegetables are tender, 3 to 4 minutes. Pour in the sesame-orange sauce, stir, and cook until hot, about 2 minutes. Stir in the arrowroot mixture and continue to cook for 1 minute, or until the sauce comes to a boil and thickens. Serve immediately over the rice, garnished with the toasted sesame seeds.

SERVES 4

A packaged rice medley, or one of your own creation, would add a special touch to this elegant sauté.

Three-Mushroom Sauté with Brandy Sauce

1 tablespoon extra virgin olive oil

1/4 cup minced onion

1 tablespoon minced carrot

1 tablespoon minced celery

1/2 teaspoon tomato paste

1 1/2 cups water

1 tablespoon tamari

1/8 teaspoon freshly ground black pepper

1 tablespoon cornstarch dissolved in 2 tablespoons water

4 ounces white mushrooms, thinly sliced (about 1 cup)

4 ounces portobello mushrooms, thinly sliced (about 1 cup)

4 ounces shiitake mushrooms, thinly sliced (about 1 cup)

2 tablespoons brandy

Salt and freshly ground black pepper to taste

4 to 5 cups hot cooked rice medley (packaged or a combination of white, brown, and wild)

1   Heat 1 1/2 teaspoons of the oil in a medium-size saucepan over medium heat. Add the onion, carrot, and celery and cook, stirring occasionally, until softened, about 5 minutes. Add the tomato paste, water, tamari, and pepper and cook, stirring frequently, for about 5 minutes, or until the liquid is reduced by one-third. Bring to a boil, whisk in the cornstarch mixture, and cook, stirring constantly, until the sauce has thickened, about 2 minutes. Remove from the heat and set aside.

2   Heat the remaining 1 1/2 teaspoons oil in a large skillet over medium-high heat. Add the mushrooms and sauté until the liquid they release has evaporated, about 4 minutes. Add the brandy and cook, stirring, for another 30 seconds. Stir in the sauce and cook until heated through, 3 to 5 minutes. Season with salt and pepper. Serve over the hot cooked rice.

SERVES 4

One taste will tell you that corn and lima beans were meant to be combined with rice. Sweet bits of red bell pepper add color, texture, and flavor to this simple sauté, which can be made with any variety of long-grain rice.

Succotash Sauté

1 tablespoon extra virgin olive oil

2 scallions, minced

1/4 cup chopped red bell pepper

4 cups cooked long-grain white, Texmati, or other rice

One 10-ounce package frozen succotash, cooked according to the package directions

1 tablespoon minced fresh Italian parsley

1/2 teaspoon salt

1/8 teaspoon freshly ground black pepper

Heat the oil in a large skillet over medium-high heat until hot. Add the scallions and bell pepper and cook, stirring, for 1 minute, or until slightly softened. Add the rice, succotash, parsley, salt, and pepper and cook, stirring occasionally, for about 8 minutes, or until heated through. Serve hot.

SERVES 4

Hoppin' John is a traditional Southern dish of rice and black-eyed peas, said to bring good luck for the New Year. It's typically served with collard greens on the side; I prefer to add them to the Hoppin' John for a nutritious one-dish meal. If collards are unavailable, kale or another dark leafy green can be substituted.

Hoppin' John with Collards

1 pound collard greens, stems trimmed

1 tablespoon extra virgin olive oil

1 medium-size onion, chopped

1½ cups cooked or canned black-eyed peas, rinsed and drained if canned

3 cups cooked long-grain white or brown rice

½ teaspoon salt

⅛ teaspoon freshly ground black pepper

Tabasco sauce to taste

1   Cook the collard greens in a large pot of boiling salted water for 10 minutes, until just tender, then rinse under cool water and drain well. Coarsely chop and set aside.

2   Heat the oil in a large skillet over medium-high heat until hot. Add the onion, cover, and cook for 5 minutes, or until soft. Add the black-eyed peas, rice, and collards and cook, stirring occasionally, for 5 minutes, or until heated through. Season with the salt and pepper and a splash of Tabasco and serve hot.

SERVES 4

Also called broccoli rabe, rapini is an assertive green that stands up to the garlic and olives in this preparation. It is a popular vegetable throughout Italy, especially in the Puglia region, where it is traditionally paired with orecchiette. For a more substantial dish, add a can of cannellini beans.

Rapini Rotini

8 ounces fresh rapini

1/4 cup extra virgin olive oil

1 garlic clove, minced

Salt to taste

1/4 teaspoon red pepper flakes

1/3 cup oil-cured black olives, pitted

1 pound rotini

Freshly grated Parmesan or soy Parmesan cheese, for serving

1. Trim the thick stems from the rapini and coarsely chop. Blanch for 3 minutes, drain, and set aside.

2. Heat 2 tablespoons of the oil in a large skillet over medium heat. Add the garlic and cook until fragrant, about 30 seconds. Add the rapini, salt, and red pepper flakes. Cook, stirring frequently, until the rapini is tender, about 5 minutes. Add the olives and keep warm over low heat.

3. Cook the rotini in a large pot of salted boiling water, stirring occasionally, until it is *al dente*. Drain and place in a large serving bowl. Add the rapini and remaining olive oil, and toss to combine. Serve immediately, with a bowl of grated cheese to pass at the table.

SERVES 4

Although carrots are widely used in the United States, parsnips and rutabagas have never achieved such popularity, perhaps because people don't know what to do with them. This colorful root vegetable sauté, with the rich nuance of toasted pecans, may change all that.

Linguine and Root Vegetable Sauté

2 carrots, cut diagonally into ¼-inch slices

2 parsnips, cut diagonally into ¼-inch slices

6 ounces rutabaga, peeled and cut into ¼-inch julienne strips

3 tablespoons extra virgin olive oil

3 shallots, halved

1 teaspoon minced fresh oregano or ½ teaspoon dried

½ teaspoon minced fresh thyme or ¼ teaspoon dried

Salt and freshly ground black pepper to taste

1 pound linguine

2 tablespoons minced fresh Italian parsley

⅓ cup chopped pecans, toasted

1   In a medium-size saucepan with a steamer insert, steam the carrots, parsnips, and rutabaga until just tender, about 5 minutes.

2   Heat the oil in a large skillet over medium heat. Add the shallots and cook until soft, about 5 minutes. Add the steamed vegetables, oregano, thyme, and salt and pepper. Cook until the vegetables begin to caramelize, about 5 minutes. Keep warm.

3   Cook the linguine in a large pot of salted boiling water, stirring occasionally, until it is *al dente*. Drain and place in a shallow serving bowl. Add the vegetable mixture and toss gently. Garnish with the parsley and pecans and serve immediately.

SERVES 4

This flavorful dish made frequent appearances on the dinner table when I was a child, where I learned early on how delicious "eating my greens" could be. Another dark, leafy green such as chicory (also known as curly endive) may be substituted for the escarole.

Escarole and Beans with Penne

1 head escarole

3 tablespoons extra virgin olive oil

3 garlic cloves, crushed

1 1/2 cups cooked or canned cannellini
   beans, rinsed and drained if canned

1/2 teaspoon salt

1/8 teaspoon freshly ground black pepper

1 pound penne

1   Bring a large pot of water to a boil. Blanch the escarole for about 2 minutes. Plunge the escarole into cold water to stop the cooking, then drain and chop coarsely.

2   Heat the oil in a large skillet over medium heat. Add the garlic and cook until fragrant, about 30 seconds. Add the escarole and cook until tender, about 5 minutes. Add the beans, salt, and pepper and simmer over low heat for about 10 minutes to blend the flavors. Keep warm.

3   Cook the penne in a large pot of salted boiling water, stirring occasionally, until it is *al dente*. Drain and place in a large serving bowl. Remove the garlic pieces from the escarole and bean mixture and discard, then add the mixture to the pasta. Toss gently and serve immediately.

SERVES 4

The slightly bitter flavor of radicchio combines well with the slightly sweet flavor of the peppers and leeks. Leeks have been paired with pasta since ancient times—an early writing of Horace refers to a dish of lasagne and chickpeas made with leeks. They are notorious for retaining sand, so be sure to wash leeks thoroughly before use.

Rigatoni with Radicchio, Italian Peppers, and Leeks

1/4 cup extra virgin olive oil

1 leek (white part only), thinly sliced

2 or 3 Italian frying peppers, or other mild pepper, thinly sliced

1 small head radicchio, coarsely chopped

1/2 teaspoon salt

1/8 teaspoon freshly ground black pepper

1 pound rigatoni

Freshly grated Pecorino Romano or soy Parmesan cheese, for serving

1   Heat 2 tablespoons of the oil in a large skillet over medium heat. Add the leek and peppers and cook until soft and slightly browned, about 7 minutes. Add the radicchio, salt, and pepper and cook until slightly softened, about 3 minutes. Keep warm.

2   Cook the rigatoni in a large pot of salted boiling water, stirring occasionally, until it is *al dente*. Drain and place in a large serving bowl. Add the vegetables and the remaining oil and toss to combine. Serve immediately, with a bowl of grated cheese to pass at the table.

SERVES 4

The raisins add a sweet counterpoint to the rest of the dish, especially the touch of hot red pepper. Including raisins and other sweet ingredients in savory recipes is a delicious Sicilian tradition. Adjust the amount of red pepper flakes used according to personal preference.

Penne with Spinach, Pine Nuts, and Raisins

1/3 cup extra virgin olive oil

2 garlic cloves, minced

1 pound fresh spinach, coarsely chopped

Salt to taste

1/4 teaspoon red pepper flakes, or to taste

1/2 cup raisins

1/4 cup pine nuts

1 pound penne

1 Heat 1 tablespoon of the oil in a large skillet over medium heat. Add the garlic, spinach, salt, and red pepper flakes. Cook until the spinach is tender, 2 to 4 minutes. Add the raisins and pine nuts and keep warm over low heat.

2 Cook the penne in a large pot of salted boiling water, stirring occasionally, until it is *al dente*. Drain and place in a large serving bowl. Add the spinach mixture and the remaining oil and toss to combine. Serve immediately.

SERVES 4

Tuscany's "straw and hay" pasta dish is so named for its green and yellow noodles. This theme is elaborated on here with the addition of green and yellow squash, cut into long strips with a mandoline slicer. If you don't have a mandoline, a sharp knife or vegetable peeler may be used.

Paglia e Fieno with Green and Yellow Squash

1/4 cup extra virgin olive oil

1 zucchini, cut into long, thin strips

1 yellow squash, cut into long, thin strips

Salt and freshly ground black pepper to taste

8 ounces spinach linguine

8 ounces regular linguine

Freshly grated Parmesan or soy Parmesan cheese

1   Heat the oil in a medium-size skillet over medium heat, add the two squashes, and cook until softened, about 5 minutes. Add salt and pepper and keep warm over low heat.

2   Cook the linguine in a large pot of salted boiling water, stirring occasionally, until it is *al dente*. Drain and place in a serving bowl. Add the squash mixture, sprinkle with cheese, and toss gently to combine. Serve immediately, with extra cheese to pass at the table.

SERVES 4

Linguine stands in for Chinese lo mein noodles in this popular noodle stir-fry. Vary the vegetables according to personal preference, substituting bok choy for the broccoli or shiitakes for the white mushrooms, if you like.

Linguine Vegetable Lo Mein

12 ounces linguine

2 teaspoons toasted sesame oil

1 tablespoon safflower oil

3 scallions, minced

1 garlic clove, minced

2 teaspoons minced fresh ginger

8 ounces extra-firm tofu, drained, blotted dry, and cut into $1/2$-inch strips

3 tablespoons tamari, or to taste

2 cups broccoli florets

$1/2$ cup thinly sliced carrots, cut diagonally

1 tablespoon water

4 ounces white mushrooms, sliced (about 1 cup)

1   Cook the linguine in a large pot of salted boiling water until it is *al dente*. Drain and place in a bowl. Add the sesame oil and toss to coat.

2   Heat the safflower oil in a large skillet or wok over medium-high heat. Add the scallions, garlic, and ginger and stir-fry until fragrant, about 30 seconds. Add the tofu and 1 tablespoon of the tamari and stir-fry until the tofu is lightly browned, about 5 minutes. Add the tofu mixture to the linguine and set aside.

3   Reheat the skillet and add the broccoli, carrots, water, and 1 tablespoon of the tamari. Stir-fry until just tender, about 5 minutes. Add the mushrooms and remaining tamari and stir-fry 1 minute longer. Add the linguine and tofu mixture to the skillet, tossing to combine, and heat through. Add additional tamari if desired and serve immediately.

SERVES 4

Stir-Fries and Sautés

Noodle stir-fries are common to virtually all Asian cuisines—the lo mein of China, Thailand's pad thai, and Indonesia's *bahmie goreng*, to name a few. This Asian fusion dish uses linguine noodles but features elements from several Asian countries, including meaty chunks of Indonesian tempeh, Chinese hoisin sauce, and Japanese sake.

Tangy Tempeh Linguine

6 tablespoons hoisin sauce

2 tablespoons tamari

2 tablespoons water

1 tablespoon sake or dry white wine

12 ounces linguine

1 teaspoon toasted sesame oil

2 tablespoons safflower oil

One 8-ounce package tempeh, cut into ½-inch cubes and poached (page 8)

1 pound bok choy, coarsely chopped (about 3 cups)

¼ cup minced shallots

1 tablespoon minced fresh ginger

¼ teaspoon red pepper flakes

1   Combine the hoisin, tamari, water, and sake in a small bowl until well blended. Set aside.

2   Cook the linguine in a large pot of salted boiling water, stirring occasionally, until it is *al dente*. Drain and place in a bowl. Add the sesame oil, toss to combine, and set aside.

3   Heat 1 tablespoon of the safflower oil in a large skillet or wok over medium-high heat. Add the tempeh and stir-fry quickly to brown it on all sides. Remove immediately with a slotted spoon. Reheat the skillet over medium heat with the remaining 1 tablespoon safflower oil. Add the bok choy, shallots, ginger, and red pepper flakes and stir for about 2 minutes, or until the bok choy is wilted. Stir in the hoisin mixture, tempeh, and linguine and cook, stirring, until heated through, about 3 minutes. Transfer to a large shallow serving bowl or individual plates and serve immediately.

SERVES 4

This popular Thai noodle dish is made here with fettuccine. It can be spiced up with the addition of hot sauce, chili paste, or red pepper flakes.

Fettuccine Pad Thai

12 ounces fettuccine

2 tablespoons safflower oil

8 ounces extra-firm tofu, drained, blotted dry, and cut into 1/2-inch strips

2 tablespoons tamari

1 small red bell pepper, cut into thin strips

1 bunch scallions, minced

1 garlic clove, minced

1 tomato, cut into eighths

2 tablespoons light brown sugar

2 tablespoons white vinegar

1/2 cup fresh bean sprouts

1/4 cup chopped peanuts

1   Cook the fettuccine in a large pot of salted boiling water, stirring occasionally, until it is *al dente*. Drain and place in a bowl. Toss with a small amount of oil and set aside.

2   Heat 1 tablespoon of the oil in a large skillet or wok over medium-high heat. Add the tofu and stir-fry until lightly browned, about 5 minutes. Splash the tofu with 1 tablespoon of the tamari, stirring to coat. Remove from the skillet and set aside.

3   Reheat the skillet over medium heat with the remaining tablespoon of oil. Add the bell pepper, scallions, and garlic and stir-fry until softened, about 5 minutes. Add the tomato, brown sugar, vinegar, and the remaining tamari. Cook for about 3 minutes to blend the flavors. Add the fettuccine and tofu and toss gently to combine and heat through. Divide among individual plates, sprinkle with bean sprouts and peanuts, and serve immediately.

SERVES 4

STOVETOP

SIMMERS

Jambalaya is traditionally made with meat or seafood and served over long-grain white rice. Since this meatless version breaks with tradition in any case, try it with brown rice instead.

Jambalaya

1 tablespoon extra virgin olive oil

1 small onion, coarsely chopped

1/2 cup coarsely chopped celery

1 green bell pepper, coarsely chopped

1 garlic clove, minced

One 14.5-ounce can diced tomatoes, drained

2 tablespoons tomato paste

1/2 teaspoon filé powder (optional)

1 tablespoon chopped fresh Italian parsley

1 teaspoon Tabasco sauce

1 teaspoon salt

1/2 cup water

1 1/2 cups cooked or canned pinto beans, rinsed and drained if canned

4 ounces poached tempeh (page 8), cut into cubes

8 ounces frozen vegetarian sausage links, cut into 1-inch pieces

4 to 5 cups hot cooked long-grain brown rice

1   In a large pot, heat 1 1/2 teaspoons of the oil over medium heat. Add the onion, celery, and bell pepper and sauté for 5 minutes, or until the vegetables begin to soften. Add the garlic, tomatoes, tomato paste, filé powder (if using), parsley, Tabasco, salt, and water. Cover and simmer for 20 minutes, or until the vegetables are soft. Stir in the beans.

2   Meanwhile, heat the remaining 1 1/2 teaspoons oil in a large skillet over medium-high heat. Add the tempeh and vegetarian sausage and cook until browned, about 5 minutes. Add the tempeh and sausage to the tomato mixture and simmer for about 10 minutes, until the flavors are well blended. Adjust the seasonings. Serve over the hot rice.

SERVES 4 TO 6

Cannellini beans and iron-rich greens make a tasty and nutritious topping for rice. You could substitute spinach, escarole, chard, or collards for the kale, or use a combination. Long-grain white or brown rice is a good choice for this dish.

Greens and Beans Ragout

1 tablespoon extra virgin olive oil

1 medium-size onion, finely chopped

2 garlic cloves, finely minced

4 cups coarsely chopped kale (or other dark leafy greens; see headnote)

½ teaspoon salt

⅛ teaspoon cayenne pepper

1 tablespoon white wine vinegar

1 cup water

3 cups cooked or canned cannellini beans, rinsed and drained if canned

4 cups hot cooked long-grain brown or white rice

1   Heat the oil in a large pot over medium heat. Add the onion and garlic and cook for 5 minutes, or until soft. Add the kale, salt, cayenne, vinegar, and water and bring to a boil. Reduce the heat, cover, and simmer over medium heat until the greens are tender, about 15 minutes.

2   Add the beans and cook, stirring, until heated through, about 5 minutes. Serve over the rice.

SERVES 4

Texmati rice, a domestic basmati hybrid, provides a fragrant base for the spicy beans, but most any variety will do. For an even quicker version of this dish, simply combine a jar of prepared salsa with the canned pinto beans in a saucepan, stir over medium heat until heated through, and serve over the rice.

Hot Salsa Pinto Beans and Rice

1 tablespoon extra virgin olive oil

1/2 cup coarsely chopped celery

1 large onion, coarsely chopped

1 green bell pepper, coarsely chopped

2 large garlic cloves, minced

One 28-ounce can diced tomatoes, drained

1 1/2 cups Vegetable Stock (page 11) or water

2 tablespoons tomato paste

1/2 teaspoon paprika

1/2 teaspoon salt

1/4 teaspoon cayenne pepper

1/8 teaspoon freshly ground black pepper

1 1/2 to 2 cups cooked or canned pinto beans, rinsed and drained if canned

2 tablespoons chopped fresh Italian parsley

1 tablespoon tamari

4 to 5 cups hot cooked Texmati, Louisiana pecan, or other rice

In a large saucepan, heat the oil over medium heat. Add the celery, onion, bell pepper, and garlic and cook, stirring occasionally, until the vegetables are soft, about 5 minutes. Add the tomatoes and stock and bring to a simmer. Stir in the tomato paste, paprika, salt, cayenne, and pepper and reduce the heat to low. Add the pinto beans, parsley, and tamari and simmer for 10 minutes. Serve over the hot rice.

SERVES 4

Tofu readily soaks up this rich homemade barbecue sauce. Long-grain white rice would be more traditional, but I prefer a fragrant jasmine, to complement the sweetness of the sauce. If vegetarian Worcestershire sauce is unavailable, use tamari instead.

Barbecued Tofu over Rice

1 small onion, coarsely chopped

1 large garlic clove, coarsely chopped

1 cup tomato sauce, store-bought or homemade

2 tablespoons fresh lemon juice

1 tablespoon vegetarian Worcestershire sauce

2 teaspoons Dijon mustard

2 tablespoons light brown sugar

1/2 teaspoon salt

1/4 teaspoon cayenne pepper

1 tablespoon extra virgin oil

1 pound extra-firm tofu, drained, blotted dry, and cut into 1/2-inch-thick slices

4 to 5 cups hot cooked jasmine or long-grain white or brown rice

1   Place the onion and garlic in a food processor and pulse until the onion is finely chopped. Add the tomato sauce, lemon juice, vegetarian Worcestershire, mustard, brown sugar, salt, and cayenne and process until smooth. Transfer the sauce mixture to a saucepan, bring to a simmer, and simmer gently, stirring occasionally, for about 30 minutes, until slightly thickened. Remove from the heat and set aside.

2   Heat the oil in a large skillet over medium-high heat. Add the tofu slices in batches, turning once, and cook until golden brown, about 5 minutes on each side.

3   Add all the tofu back to the skillet, add the barbecue sauce to the tofu, bring to a simmer, and simmer for about 10 minutes, spooning the sauce over the tofu to coat well. Serve over the hot rice.

SERVES 4

Additional orange juice can be substituted for the Grand Marnier in this tasty sauce. I recommend flavorful brown Texmati or Louisiana pecan rice, but feel free to experiment.

Orange-Glazed Tofu Strips over Rice

1 tablespoon safflower oil

1 pound extra-firm tofu, drained, blotted dry, and cut into 1/4-inch-wide strips

Salt and freshly ground black pepper to taste

1/2 cup fresh orange juice

1/4 cup Grand Marnier or other orange liqueur

1 garlic clove, minced

1/4 cup golden raisins

1 1/2 tablespoons tomato paste

1 tablespoon Dijon mustard

1 teaspoon sugar

1/2 cup water

1 tablespoon cornstarch dissolved in 2 tablespoons water

1 teaspoon fresh lemon juice

4 to 6 cups hot cooked brown Texmati, Louisiana pecan, or other rice

1   Heat the oil in a large skillet over medium-high heat. Add the tofu and sauté until golden brown, about 10 minutes. Season with salt and pepper, remove from the heat, and set aside in the skillet.

2   In a small saucepan, combine the orange juice, Grand Marnier, garlic, and raisins and bring to a boil. Reduce the heat to medium, stir in the tomato paste, mustard, sugar, and water, and simmer for 5 minutes or until slightly syrupy. Stir in the cornstarch mixture, stirring to thicken, about 1 minute. Add the lemon juice. Pour the sauce over the tofu and simmer until the tofu is heated through and glazed with sauce, about 5 minutes. Serve over the hot rice.

SERVES 4

Cumin, cilantro, and jalapeños add a decidedly Southwestern accent to this Southern favorite. For a variation, add a can of diced tomatoes along with the beans.

Cumin-Spiced Red Beans and Rice

1 tablespoon extra virgin oil

1 small onion, finely minced

1 small green bell pepper, chopped

1 or 2 jalapeño chiles, seeded and minced

$1/2$ cup chopped celery

2 large garlic cloves, minced

1 teaspoon ground cumin

$1/2$ teaspoon paprika

$1/4$ teaspoon dried oregano

$1/2$ teaspoon salt, or to taste

$1/8$ teaspoon cayenne pepper, or to taste

$1/8$ teaspoon freshly ground black pepper, or to taste

3 cups cooked or canned dark red kidney beans (adzuki or pinto beans can be substituted), rinsed and drained if canned

4 cups hot cooked Texmati, Louisiana pecan, or long-grain rice

2 tablespoons minced fresh cilantro, for garnish

Heat the oil in a large skillet over medium heat. Add the onion, bell pepper, jalapeños, celery, garlic, cumin, paprika, oregano, salt, cayenne, and black pepper and cook, stirring occasionally, until the vegetables are softened and lightly browned, about 10 minutes. Add the beans and cook 10 minutes longer, stirring occasionally, to allow the flavors to blend. Taste and adjust the seasoning. Serve the beans on top of the rice, sprinkled with the cilantro.

SERVES 4

This delicious recipe offers interesting variations. For an Eastern European accent, omit the cinnamon and add caraway seeds. For a taste of India, stir some curry powder into the cabbage and onion.

Rice and Cabbage with Apples and Raisins

1 tablespoon safflower oil

1/2 cup minced onion

2 cups shredded green cabbage

1 1/4 cups basmati rice (or rice of your choice)

1 Granny Smith apple, diced

2 tablespoons golden raisins

2 cups water

1/2 teaspoon ground cinnamon

Salt and freshly ground black pepper to taste

Heat the oil in a large saucepan over medium heat. Add the onion and cabbage and cook, stirring occasionally, until softened, about 5 minutes. Stir in the rice, apple, and raisins and cook for 1 minute. Stir in the water and cinnamon and bring to a boil over high heat. Reduce the heat to low, cover, and simmer until all the liquid is absorbed and the rice is tender, 20 to 25 minutes. Season with salt and pepper and serve.

SERVES 4

Fresh sage and white beans are a classic Italian combination. Here the dusky flavor of the herb permeates a delicate white bean sauce. Try it on a rice medley—it goes especially well with the slightly nutty flavors of long-grain brown and wild rice.

Rice with Sage-Infused White Bean Sauce

2 tablespoons extra virgin olive oil

1 carrot, finely chopped

1 medium-size onion, minced

1 garlic clove, minced

1 tablespoon chopped fresh sage or 1 teaspoon dried

1½ cups cooked or canned Great Northern beans or other white beans, rinsed and drained if canned

2 to 3 cups Vegetable Stock (page 11) or water

Salt and freshly ground black pepper to taste

4 to 5 cups hot cooked rice medley (packaged or a combination of your choice)

2 tablespoons chopped fresh Italian parsley, for garnish

1   In a large saucepan, heat the oil over medium heat. Add the carrot, onion, garlic, and sage and sauté until the onion is soft, about 5 minutes. Add the beans and 2 cups stock, bring to a simmer, and simmer for about 20 minutes, or until the liquid reduces slightly and the vegetables are very soft.

2   Transfer the bean mixture to a food processor and puree until almost smooth. Transfer the bean puree to a saucepan, season with salt and pepper, and stir in up to 1 cup more stock to make a smooth, thick sauce. Reheat the sauce over low heat and serve over the hot rice, sprinkled with the parsley.

SERVES 4

One of my favorite ways to enjoy rice is topped with the famous Cajun stew called *étouffée*, which translates from the French as "smothered." Although there are many variations on this classic dish, étouffée is usually made with crawfish or shrimp. This brimming-with-vegetables version still has that great New Orleans taste because it's based on a dark roux, the traditional butter-and-flour thickener (although olive oil stands in for butter here), and the famous Cajun "trinity" of onion, celery, and bell pepper. The ingredients list may seem long, but this stew cooks in only 30 minutes.

Vegetable Etouffée

¼ cup all-purpose flour

1½ tablespoons extra virgin olive oil

1 medium-size onion, finely chopped

1 celery rib, finely chopped

1 green bell pepper, finely chopped

2 zucchini, halved lengthwise and cut into ½-inch slices

2 garlic cloves, minced

2 cups water

One 14.5-ounce can tomato puree

1 teaspoon dried thyme

½ teaspoon filé powder

1 bay leaf

Salt and freshly ground black pepper to taste

¼ teaspoon cayenne pepper

1½ cups cooked or canned kidney beans, rinsed and drained if canned

3 scallions, chopped

2 tablespoons minced fresh Italian parsley

Hot pepper sauce to taste (optional)

4 to 5 cups hot cooked long-grain white, Louisiana pecan, or other rice

1   Heat a large skillet over medium heat. Add the flour and stir constantly until it turns light brown, 3 to 5 minutes; do not let burn. Transfer the flour to a small plate and set aside.

2   Heat the oil in the same skillet over medium heat. Add the onion, celery, bell pepper, zucchini, and garlic, cover, and cook for 10 minutes, or until soft. Add the browned flour, stirring to coat the vegetables. Add the water, tomato puree, thyme, filé powder, bay leaf, salt and pepper, and cayenne, bring to a simmer, and simmer over low heat for 10 minutes, stirring occasionally, until thickened. Add the beans, scallions, and parsley and cook for 5 minutes longer, or until heated through. Taste and adjust the seasoning, adding a splash of hot pepper sauce if desired. Serve over the hot rice.

SERVES 4

Spanakorizo, or "spinach rice," can be made with either long- or short-grain rice, depending on your preference for the texture of the dish, but I prefer the appearance of the fluffy separate grains of long-grain varieties here. Try it garnished with chopped ripe tomatoes or regular or soy crumbled feta, or both.

Greek Rice and Spinach

1 tablespoon extra virgin olive oil

1 small onion, finely chopped

4 cups chopped fresh spinach

1½ cups long-grain white rice

3 cups Vegetable Stock (page 11) or water

1 teaspoon minced fresh oregano or ½ teaspoon dried

½ teaspoon salt

⅛ teaspoon freshly ground black pepper

Pinch of ground nutmeg

3 tablespoons chopped fresh mint

1   Heat the oil in a large skillet over medium heat. Add the onion and cook for 5 minutes, or until softened. Add the spinach and cook until wilted, about 2 minutes. Add the rice, stock, oregano, salt, pepper, and nutmeg and bring to a boil. Reduce the heat to low, cover, and simmer for 20 minutes, or until the rice is tender and all the liquid has been absorbed.

2   Stir in the mint, remove from the heat, and allow to stand for 5 minutes. Fluff with a fork and serve.

SERVES 4

This flavorful Moroccan stew is named for the earthenware pot in which it is cooked. It is traditionally made with meat, preserved lemons or other fruit, and heady spices. Here, chickpeas stand in for the meat. Tagines are usually served with couscous, but rice—almost any variety of rice could be enjoyed with this dish—makes a nice change of pace.

Vegetable Tagine

1 tablespoon extra virgin olive oil

1 large onion, chopped

1 carrot, chopped

1 zucchini, diced

1 garlic clove, minced

1/2 teaspoon ground cinnamon

1/2 teaspoon ground turmeric

1/4 teaspoon cayenne pepper

One 14.5-ounce can diced tomatoes, drained

2 cups Vegetable Stock (page 11) or water

Salt to taste

1/2 cup dried apricots

1/4 cup raisins

Zest of 1 lemon

3 cups cooked or canned chickpeas, rinsed and drained if canned

2 tablespoons minced fresh cilantro or Italian parsley

4 to 5 cups hot cooked brown basmati or other rice

1   Heat the oil in a large saucepan over medium heat. Add the onion and carrot and cook, covered, for 5 minutes, or until softened. Add the zucchini, garlic, cinnamon, turmeric, cayenne, tomatoes, stock, and salt. Reduce the heat to low, and simmer for 25 minutes.

2   Meanwhile, soak the apricots in hot water for 20 minutes, then drain and finely chop. Add the apricots, raisins, lemon zest, and chickpeas to the vegetable mixture and cook 5 minutes longer, or until hot and the flavors are blended. Stir in the cilantro and serve over the rice.

SERVES 4

This recipe was inspired by a Nigerian dish called *wake-ewa*, which is made with black-eyed peas. I like to serve it over short-grain brown rice to complement the robust flavors of the dish, but any rice can be used.

Nigerian Black-Eyed Peas

1 tablespoon extra virgin olive oil

1 large onion, chopped

1 teaspoon chili powder

1 teaspoon dried thyme

1 teaspoon ground coriander

One 14.5-ounce can diced tomatoes, drained

$^1/_2$ teaspoon sugar

Salt to taste

$1^1/_2$ to 2 cups cooked or canned black-eyed peas, rinsed and drained if canned

4 to 5 cups hot cooked short-grain brown, brown basmati, or other rice

Heat the oil in a large skillet over medium heat. Add the onion and cook for 5 minutes, or until softened. Stir in the chili powder, thyme, coriander, tomatoes, sugar, and salt. Reduce the heat to low and simmer for 5 minutes, stirring frequently; add a little water if the mixture becomes too dry. Add the black-eyed peas and cook 5 minutes longer to heat through and blend the flavors. Serve over the hot rice.

SERVES 4

Red pepper, carrots, and zucchini add color, texture, and flavor to this creamy risotto. Serve it in shallow soup bowls, with a crisp salad and warm garlic bread for a satisfying meal. While Arborio rice is the most readily available in the United States, Carnaroli and Vialone nano are also highly prized risotto rices.

Risotto Primavera

4 1/2 cups Vegetable Stock (page 11) or water

1 tablespoon extra virgin olive oil

1/2 cup finely chopped red bell pepper

1/2 cup grated carrots

1 cup shredded zucchini

2 garlic cloves, minced

1 1/2 cups Arborio rice

1/4 cup dry white wine

Salt and freshly ground black pepper to taste

1/4 cup chopped fresh Italian parsley

1 tablespoon fresh lemon juice

1   In a medium-size saucepan, bring the stock to a simmer, reduce the heat to low, and keep at a simmer.

2   Heat the olive oil in a large saucepan over medium heat until hot. Add the bell pepper, carrots, zucchini, and garlic and sauté for 5 minutes. Add the rice, and stir to coat with oil. Add the wine and simmer gently, stirring occasionally, until it has been absorbed.

3   Add 1/2 cup of the hot stock and cook, stirring constantly, until all the liquid has been absorbed. Adjust the heat as necessary to maintain a simmer. Continue cooking, adding stock 1/2 cup at a time and stirring until it is absorbed, until the rice is tender but still firm and the risotto is thick and creamy, about 25 minutes (you may not need all the stock). Add salt and pepper, then add the parsley and lemon juice. Adjust the seasoning if necessary. Serve immediately.

SERVES 4

Italian porcini mushrooms, also called cèpes, add a rich flavor and an authentic touch to this elegant risotto. Although expensive, the results are well worth it. These mushrooms are available seasonally at specialty markets and many well-stocked supermarkets. If unavailable, substitute creminis, portobellos, or white button mushrooms.

Risotto with Artichokes and Mushrooms

4 cups Vegetable Stock (page 11) or water

2 tablespoons extra virgin olive oil

1 small onion, minced

1½ cups Arborio rice

¼ cup dry white wine

4 ounces porcini or other mushrooms, chopped (about 1 cup)

1 cup cooked frozen or canned artichoke hearts, chopped

½ teaspoon salt

Freshly ground black pepper to taste

1   In a medium-size saucepan, bring the stock to a simmer, reduce the heat to low, and keep at a simmer.

2   In a large saucepan, heat the oil over medium heat. Add the onion and sauté, stirring frequently, until soft and golden brown, about 5 minutes. Add the rice and mushrooms and stir until coated with oil and the rice turns translucent. Sauté for 5 minutes and stir to coat with oil. Add the wine and simmer gently, stirring occasionally, until it has been absorbed.

3   Add ½ cup of the stock and cook, stirring constantly, until all the liquid has been absorbed. Adjust the heat as necessary to maintain a simmer. Continue cooking, adding stock ½ cup at a time and stirring until it is absorbed, until the rice is tender but still firm and the risotto is thick and creamy, about 25 minutes (you may not need all the stock).

4   About 10 minutes before the rice is finished, stir in the artichoke hearts. When the risotto is finished, remove from the heat and season with the salt and pepper. Serve immediately in shallow bowls.

SERVES 4

Stovetop Simmers

Easier than a risotto, this classic rice and pea combination, made with Arborio rice, is a favorite Italian comfort food. For added flavor, top with finely chopped lightly browned vegetarian Canadian bacon, available at natural foods stores and many supermarkets.

Risi e Bisi

1 tablespoon extra virgin olive oil	1/2 teaspoon salt
1/2 cup minced onion	1/8 teaspoon freshly ground black pepper
1 1/4 cups Arborio rice	1 1/2 cups fresh or frozen green peas
3 3/4 cups Vegetable Stock (page 11) or water	1 tablespoon chopped fresh Italian parsley, for garnish

1   Heat the olive oil in a large skillet over medium heat. Add the onion and cook until softened, about 5 minutes. Reduce the heat to low. Stir in the rice, stock, salt, and pepper, bring to a simmer, and simmer for 20 minutes, stirring frequently.

2   Add the peas and cook, stirring frequently, for 5 minutes longer, or until the rice is soft. Adjust the seasoning if necessary, sprinkle with the chopped parsley, and serve.

SERVES 4

The firm, meaty texture of tempeh makes it well suited as the substitute for chicken in this vegetarian version of the Spanish classic *arroz con pollo*.

Arroz con Tempeh

1 tablespoon extra virgin olive oil

8 ounces poached tempeh (page 8), cut into 1-inch pieces

1 medium-size onion, chopped

1 red bell pepper, chopped

1 small carrot, chopped

2 garlic cloves, chopped

1/2 teaspoon dried oregano

1/2 teaspoon ground cumin

1/8 teaspoon saffron threads or ground turmeric

1 1/4 cups Valencia or other short-grain rice

One 14.5-ounce can diced tomatoes

3 1/2 cups Vegetable Stock (page 11) or water

8 ounces green beans, ends trimmed and cut into 1-inch pieces (2 cups)

Salt to taste

1/2 cup frozen peas, thawed

1/3 cup pimiento-stuffed green olives

1/4 cup tomato salsa, store-bought or homemade (page 81)

Freshly ground black pepper to taste

1   Heat the oil in a large saucepan over medium heat. Add the tempeh, onion, bell pepper, and carrot. Cover, and cook for 5 minutes, or until the vegetables are softened. Add the garlic, oregano, cumin, and saffron and sauté for 1 to 2 minutes longer. Stir in the rice, then add the tomatoes, stock, green beans, and salt. Cover, and simmer for 20 to 25 minutes, or until the rice is tender.

2   Add the peas, olives, and salsa, season with pepper, and cook for about 5 minutes, until heated through. Taste and adjust the seasonings before serving hot.

SERVES 4

Ratatouille, the classic vegetable stew from Provence, makes a perfect topping for rice. And since ratatouille, like many stews, tastes even better the day after it's made, make both it and your rice ahead, for a convenient meal that's ready to heat up in a flash. Any rice or other grain tastes great topped with this flavorful mélange, so feel free to experiment.

Provençal Vegetables and Rice

1 tablespoon extra virgin olive oil

1 small eggplant, cut into ½-inch cubes

1 medium-size onion, diced

1 red bell pepper, cut into ½-inch pieces

2 garlic cloves, minced

2 small zucchini, cut into ½-inch cubes

2 cups chopped fresh or canned tomatoes

2 tablespoons chopped fresh Italian parsley

1 tablespoon chopped fresh basil

1 teaspoon minced fresh thyme

1 teaspoon salt

⅛ teaspoon cayenne pepper

4 to 5 cups hot cooked rice

Heat the oil in a large saucepan over medium heat. Add the eggplant and onion, cover, and cook for 5 minutes, or until softened. Add the bell pepper and garlic, cover, and cook, stirring occasionally, for 5 minutes longer or until soft. Add the zucchini, tomatoes, parsley, basil, thyme, salt, and cayenne and cook for 20 minutes, or until all the vegetables are tender. Taste and adjust the seasoning. Serve over the hot cooked rice.

SERVES 4

The Spanish name for this classic Cuban dish is *moros y cristianos*, or "Moors and Christians." My version is ready in minutes with the help of canned black beans and already cooked rice. For authenticity, use a long-grain white rice.

Cuban Black Beans and Rice

1 tablespoon extra virgin olive oil

1 medium-size onion, finely chopped

¹/₂ green bell pepper, minced

2 garlic cloves, minced

1 jalapeño chile (optional), seeded and minced

¹/₂ teaspoon ground cumin

¹/₄ teaspoon dried oregano

One 14.5-ounce can diced tomatoes, drained

3 cups cooked or canned black beans, rinsed and drained if canned

¹/₂ teaspoon salt

Freshly ground black pepper to taste

4 cups hot cooked long-grain white rice

Heat the oil in a large saucepan over medium heat. Add the onion, bell pepper, garlic, and jalapeño, if using, cover, and cook for 5 minutes, or until the vegetables begin to soften. Stir in the cumin and oregano and cook for 1 minute, or until fragrant. Add the tomatoes, beans, salt, and pepper, cover, and simmer, stirring occasionally, for 15 minutes, or until the vegetables are tender. Taste and adjust the seasoning, spoon over the hot rice, and serve.

SERVES 4

Tempeh replaces ground beef in this Mexican favorite, which combines sweet apples and raisins with olives, garlic, and hot chiles for a symphony of flavors and textures. Various brands of crumbled vegetarian burgers are available in supermarkets and natural foods stores and can be substituted for the tempeh. Long-grain white rice is traditional with picadillo.

Tempeh Picadillo

1 tablespoon extra virgin olive oil

1 medium-size onion, chopped

1 small green bell pepper, minced

8 ounces poached tempeh (see page 8), grated

2 garlic cloves, chopped

1 jalapeño chile, chopped

One 14.5-ounce can diced tomatoes, undrained

1 Granny Smith apple, peeled and chopped

1/2 cup raisins

1/4 cup sliced pitted black olives

Salt and freshly ground black pepper to taste

3 1/2 cups hot cooked long-grain white, Texmati, or other rice

2 tablespoons chopped fresh Italian parsley, for garnish

2 tablespoons toasted slivered almonds, for garnish

1   Heat the oil in a large skillet over medium heat. Add the onion, bell pepper, tempeh, garlic, and chile and cook, stirring occasionally, for 5 minutes, or until the vegetables are soft and the tempeh is golden brown. Stir in the tomatoes and their juice, apple, raisins, olives, and salt and pepper. Simmer for 15 minutes, stirring occasionally, until the flavors are well blended. Add a little water if the mixture becomes too dry.

2   To serve, stir the rice into the tempeh mixture, transfer to a large shallow serving bowl, and garnish with the chopped parsley and slivered almonds.

SERVES 4

Chickpeas and rice, a favorite Indian combination, are featured in this spicy mélange, which also includes cabbage and carrots. Other vegetables, such as broccoli, cauliflower, or peas, may be added or substituted to suit personal taste.

Indian-Spiced Vegetables over Basmati Rice

1 tablespoon safflower oil

1 large onion, thinly sliced

2 garlic cloves, minced

1 tablespoon minced fresh ginger

2 large carrots, cut on the diagonal into $1/4$-inch slices

3 cups shredded napa cabbage

$1^1/2$ cups cooked or canned chickpeas, rinsed and drained if canned

$3/4$ teaspoon ground cardamom

$1/4$ teaspoon ground cinnamon

$1/4$ teaspoon ground turmeric

$1/2$ teaspoon salt

$1/8$ teaspoon cayenne pepper

$1/2$ cup water

1 cup unsweetened coconut milk

4 to 5 cups hot cooked basmati rice

1 Heat the oil in a large skillet over medium heat. Add the onion, garlic, and ginger and cook until the onion is soft and lightly browned, about 7 minutes. Add the carrots, cabbage, chickpeas, cardamom, cinnamon, turmeric, salt, and cayenne. Cover and cook for 5 minutes, or until the vegetables are softened. Add the water and bring to a boil. Reduce the heat, cover, and simmer for about 15 minutes, or until the vegetables are tender.

2 Stir in the coconut milk and heat through. Taste and adjust the seasonings if necessary. Serve over the hot cooked rice.

SERVES 4

A traditional combination in India and the Middle East, lentils and rice make this wholesome and simple, but subtly spiced, dish a powerhouse of protein. Accompany with a salad or leafy green vegetable.

Rice and Lentils

1 cup brown lentils, rinsed and picked over

1 tablespoon extra virgin olive oil

1 large onion, minced

1 teaspoon ground cumin

1 teaspoon ground coriander

1 teaspoon minced fresh ginger

Salt and freshly ground black pepper to taste

1 cup basmati rice

3 cups water

1   Bring a large saucepan of water to a boil, add the lentils, and cook for 10 minutes.

2   Meanwhile, heat the oil in a large skillet over medium-high heat. Add the onion and cook, stirring frequently, until lightly browned, 7 to 10 minutes. Stir in the cumin, coriander, and ginger. Remove from the heat.

3   Drain the lentils, return them to the saucepan, and add the cooked onion mixture. Season with salt and pepper. Add the rice and 3 cups water, bring to a boil, reduce the heat, and simmer, covered, for about 20 minutes, until the lentils and rice are tender. Remove from the heat and allow to stand for 10 minutes before serving.

SERVES 4

Small, slender Japanese eggplants, available in many well-stocked supermarkets and in Asian grocery stores, are best for this dish. Almost any variety of rice will complement the flavors of the teriyaki sauce.

Japanese Eggplant Teriyaki

4 small Japanese eggplants, quartered lengthwise

1 garlic clove, minced

3 tablespoons fresh lemon juice

3 tablespoons tamari

1 tablespoon light brown sugar

2 tablespoons toasted sesame oil

1 tablespoon safflower oil

4 to 5 cups hot cooked rice

1   Place the eggplant quarters in a large shallow dish and pierce the skin of each in several places with a fork. In a small bowl, whisk together the garlic, lemon juice, tamari, and brown sugar. Add the sesame oil in a slow, steady stream, whisking constantly until the mixture is emulsified and smooth. Pour the marinade over the eggplant, turning the eggplant to coat well. Allow the eggplant to marinate, turning occasionally, for at least 1 hour, or overnight in the refrigerator.

2   When ready to cook, remove the eggplant from the marinade, reserving the marinade. Heat the safflower oil in a large skillet over medium heat. Add the eggplant and cook, turning once, until softened and browned on both sides, about 4 minutes. Add the reserved marinade and simmer, turning the eggplant once, for about 10 minutes, or until the eggplant is tender and the sauce is syrupy. Serve over the rice.

SERVES 4

The heady intensity of Jamaican jerk spices are readily absorbed by the tempeh, making this dish especially flavorful. Serve over rice or couscous, with chutney and chopped peanuts as accompaniments.

Jamaican Jerk Tempeh

3 tablespoons ground chiles

1 teaspoon ground cinnamon

1 teaspoon ground allspice

1 teaspoon dried oregano

1 teaspoon ground cumin

2 teaspoons light brown sugar

1/4 teaspoon cayenne pepper

1/4 teaspoon ground nutmeg

1/4 teaspoon ground coriander

1 pound poached tempeh (page 8), diced

2 tablespoons extra virgin olive oil

3 garlic cloves

1 medium-size onion, minced

1 zucchini, halved lengthwise and thinly sliced

One 28-ounce can diced tomatoes, drained

1 cup water

1 tablespoon rum

1 tablespoon tamari

Salt to taste

1   In a small bowl, combine the chiles, cinnamon, allspice, oregano, cumin, brown sugar, cayenne, nutmeg, and coriander. Add the tempeh and toss to coat.

2   Heat 1 tablespoon of the oil in a large skillet over medium heat. Add the tempeh pieces (reserving any remaining spice mixture) and cook until lightly browned, about 5 minutes. Set aside.

3   Heat the remaining tablespoon of oil in a large stockpot over medium heat. Add the garlic, onion, and zucchini, cover, and cook until softened, about 10 minutes. Add the reserved tempeh and tomatoes and stir to combine. Add the reserved spice mixture along with the water, rum, and tamari. Bring to a boil, lower the heat, add the salt, and simmer until the flavors are blended, about 30 minutes. Serve hot.

SERVES 4

The apple juice and allspice add a spicy sweetness to this exotic-tasting dish. Couscous can be ready in minutes, so if you've made the chickpeas in advance, this can truly be a "fast-food" meal.

Moroccan Chickpeas with Couscous

1 tablespoon extra virgin olive oil

1 medium-size onion, chopped

1 jalapeño chile, minced

3 garlic cloves, minced

1 teaspoon dried marjoram

1/2 teaspoon allspice

One 28-ounce can diced tomatoes, drained

2 cups apple juice

3 cups cooked or canned chickpeas, rinsed and drained if canned

One 12-ounce package frozen vegetarian burger crumbles

1 cup frozen green peas, thawed

Salt to taste

4 to 5 cups cooked couscous

2 tablespoons minced scallions, for garnish

1   Heat the oil in a large stockpot over medium heat. Add the onion, jalapeño, and garlic, cover, and cook until softened, about 5 minutes. Add the marjoram and allspice. Stir in the tomatoes and apple juice. Lower the heat and simmer, covered, for 20 minutes, stirring occasionally.

2   Add the chickpeas, vegetarian burger crumbles, peas, and salt, and simmer 10 minutes longer, or until the desired consistency is reached. Serve over couscous, and garnish with the minced scallions.

SERVES 4

Serve this fragrant, Indian-style mélange over basmati rice accompanied by small bowls of curry garnishes, such as regular or soy yogurt or sour cream, minced scallions, chopped peanuts, and chutney.

Zesty Bombay Beans with Chutney

2 tablespoons extra virgin olive oil

1 large onion, chopped

2 garlic cloves, minced

8 ounces green beans, ends trimmed and cut into 1-inch pieces (2 cups)

1 red bell pepper, diced

1 jalapeño chile (optional), minced

1 tablespoon curry powder

1/2 teaspoon ground cumin

1/2 teaspoon ground red chiles

1/2 teaspoon ground coriander

One 6-ounce can tomato paste

One 28-ounce can diced tomatoes, drained

3 cups cooked or canned red kidney beans, rinsed and drained if canned

1 teaspoon salt

1 1/2 cups water

1/2 cup spicy sweet chutney

1   Heat the oil in a large stockpot over medium heat. Add the onion, garlic, green beans, bell pepper, and jalapeño (if using), cover, and cook until softened, about 5 minutes. Stir in the curry powder, cumin, chiles, coriander, and tomato paste. Add the tomatoes, kidney beans, salt, and water. Bring to a boil, lower the heat, and simmer for 30 minutes.

2   Stir in the chutney and simmer 10 minutes longer, or until desired consistency is reached. Serve hot.

SERVES 6

HEARTY

CHILIS

Try one of the rices from the Lundberg Family Farm in this zesty chili: Texmati, their basmati hybrid, or Wehani, a mellow brown rice, are both good choices, each adding its own particular nuance. If you put the rice on to cook as you begin to assemble the chili ingredients, everything should be ready at the same time.

Quick Veggie Chili over Texmati Rice

1½ cups Texmati or Wehani rice

3 cups water

Salt to taste

1 tablespoon extra virgin olive oil

1 medium-size onion, chopped

1 green bell pepper, chopped

1 garlic clove, minced

3 tablespoons chili powder, or more to taste

3 cups cooked or canned pinto beans, rinsed and drained if canned

One 14.5-ounce can diced tomatoes, drained

One 14.5-ounce can crushed tomatoes

One 16-ounce can corn kernels, drained

Freshly ground black pepper to taste

1   In a medium-size saucepan, combine the rice, water, and ½ teaspoon salt and bring to a boil. Reduce the heat, cover, and simmer for 20 to 40 minutes (depending on the type of rice), until the rice is tender.

2   While the rice is cooking, heat the oil in a large skillet over low heat. Add the onion, bell pepper, garlic, and chili powder and cook, covered, for 10 minutes, or until the vegetables are tender. Remove the cover, stir in 1½ cups water, beans, diced tomatoes, crushed tomatoes, corn, and salt and pepper to taste, and cook for 20 minutes, or until the desired consistency is reached. Serve over the hot rice.

SERVES 4

The vivid contrast of the black beans and bright orange pumpkin makes this chili a perfect party food at Halloween time. Make it the centerpiece of your table by serving it in a large, hollowed-out pumpkin or an old cast-iron "cauldron."

Pumpkin and Black Bean Chili

2 pounds pumpkin or butternut squash, peeled and seeded

1 tablespoon extra virgin olive oil

1 large onion, chopped

1 garlic clove, minced

1 jalapeño chile, minced

One 14.5-ounce can diced tomatoes, drained

One 14.5-ounce can crushed tomatoes

1 cup water

1 cup apple juice

4 tablespoons chili powder

1 teaspoon salt

1/8 teaspoon cayenne pepper

3 cups cooked or canned black beans, rinsed and drained if canned

1   Cut the pumpkin into 1/2-inch chunks and set aside.

2   Heat the oil in a large pot over medium heat. Add the onion, garlic, and jalapeño. Cover, and cook, stirring occasionally, until softened, about 10 minutes. Add the reserved pumpkin, diced tomatoes, crushed tomatoes, water, apple juice, chili powder, salt, and cayenne, and stir well. Bring to a boil, lower the heat, cover, and simmer until the pumpkin is tender, about 30 minutes.

3   Add the beans, and more water if the chili is too thick for your taste. Cover, and continue to simmer about 15 minutes to blend flavors. Serve hot.

SERVES 4 TO 6

Chayote is a small, light green pear-shaped squash, native to Mexico and Central America. Its delicate flavor complements the spiciness of the chili seasonings. I like the dramatic color contrast of the pale green chayote and the deep red kidney beans.

Chili with Chayote

1 pound chayote, halved and seeded

1 tablespoon extra virgin olive oil

1 large onion, chopped

2 garlic cloves, minced

1 jalapeño chile, seeded and minced

1 small green bell pepper, chopped

3 cups cooked or canned dark red kidney beans, rinsed and drained if canned

One 28-ounce can crushed tomatoes

3 tablespoons chili powder

1 teaspoon ground cumin

2 tablespoons vegetarian Worcestershire sauce

2 cups water

3/4 teaspoon salt

1/8 teaspoon freshly ground black pepper

Low-fat sour cream or tofu sour cream, for serving

Hot or mild salsa, store-bought or homemade, for serving

1   Cut the chayote into 1/2-inch cubes and set aside.

2   Heat the oil in a large pot over medium heat. Add the onion, garlic, and jalapeño, cover, and cook until softened, about 5 minutes. Add the chayote and bell pepper, cover, and continue cooking until the vegetables soften, about 10 minutes. Add the beans, tomatoes, chili powder, cumin, Worcestershire, water, and salt and pepper. Bring to a boil, lower the heat, and simmer, uncovered, for 30 minutes.

3   Serve hot, accompanied by small bowls of sour cream and salsa to use as toppings.

SERVES 4 TO 6

This "green chili" is a St. Patrick's Day tradition in our house. I serve
it over green spinach rotini and top it with guacamole for a truly
cross-cultural celebration. Fresh tomatillos look like small green
tomatoes in papery husks. They have a slightly tart flavor. If
unavailable, use the canned variety. Salsa verde, a green salsa,
is available in most supermarkets.

Chili Verde

1 tablespoon extra virgin olive oil

1 medium-size onion, chopped

2 garlic cloves, minced

1 large green bell pepper, chopped

2 or 3 green tomatoes, chopped

1 1/2 cups husked and chopped tomatillos,
or one 14-ounce can tomatillos, drained
and chopped

1 cup salsa verde, store-bought or
homemade

1 teaspoon dried oregano, preferably
Mexican

3/4 teaspoon ground cumin

1 teaspoon sugar

Salt and freshly ground black pepper to
taste

1 1/2 cups water

3 cups cooked or canned Great Northern
beans or other white beans, rinsed and
drained if canned

One 4-ounce can diced mild green chiles,
drained

1/4 cup chopped fresh Italian parsley, for
garnish

1/4 cup chopped fresh cilantro, for garnish

1   Heat the oil in a large pot over medium heat. Add the onion, garlic, bell pepper, and
tomatoes. Cover, and cook until the vegetables begin to soften, about 5 minutes. Add
the tomatillos, salsa verde, oregano, cumin, sugar, and salt and pepper.

2   Lower the heat, add the water, beans, and chiles, and simmer, stirring often, until the
mixture is thickened and the vegetables are tender, about 40 minutes, adding more
water if the chili becomes too dry. Garnish each serving with the chopped parsley and
cilantro.

SERVES 4 TO 6

The anasazi is a sweet, meaty bean, the name of which means "the ancient ones" in the Navajo language. Paired with fresh-cooked quinoa, the high-protein grain of the ancient Incas, it becomes a dish steeped in Native American heritage. If anasazi beans are unavailable, use pinto or kidney beans.

Anasazi Chili with Quinoa

1 tablespoon extra virgin olive oil

1 large onion, finely chopped

1 red bell pepper, chopped

3 tablespoons chili powder, commercial or homemade

1 teaspoon ground cumin

1 teaspoon dried oregano, preferably Mexican

1 teaspoon salt

1/8 teaspoon freshly ground black pepper

3 cups chopped fresh or canned plum tomatoes

3 cups cooked or canned anasazi beans, rinsed and drained if canned

1 1/2 cups water

4 cups hot cooked quinoa

Heat the oil in a large pot over medium heat. Add the onion and bell pepper, cover, and cook until the onion is softened, about 5 minutes. Add the chili powder, cumin, oregano, and salt and pepper. Stir to blend. Add the tomatoes, anasazi beans, and water. Bring to a boil, lower the heat, and simmer for 30 minutes, stirring occasionally. Taste, and adjust the seasonings. Spoon the chili over the hot quinoa.

SERVES 4

No, tempeh is not a city in Arizona—it's compressed soybeans formed into cakes. Tempeh's meat-like texture and high protein content make it a natural ingredient for vegetarian chili.

Tex-Mex Tempeh Chili

2 tablespoons extra virgin olive oil

1 large onion, chopped

2 garlic cloves, minced

1 pound poached tempeh (page 8), diced

3 to 4 tablespoons hot or mild chili powder

1 teaspoon ground cumin

1 teaspoon dried oregano, preferably Mexican

One 28-ounce can crushed tomatoes

One 4-ounce can diced mild green chiles, drained

1 cup water

Salt and freshly ground black pepper to taste

1 cup canned or frozen corn kernels

1   Heat the oil in a large pot over medium heat. Add the onion and garlic, and cover and cook, stirring frequently, until the onion is softened, about 10 minutes. Stir in the tempeh and cook 5 minutes longer. Add the chili powder, cumin, oregano, tomatoes, chiles, water, and salt and pepper. Bring to a boil, lower the heat, and simmer for 30 minutes, stirring occasionally.

2   Add the corn, taste, and adjust the seasonings. Cook 10 minutes longer, or until the desired consistency is reached.

SERVES 4

Chili is served in this manner throughout Cincinnati: "two-way" is served over spaghetti, "three-way" adds cheese, and "four-way" adds chopped onion to the cheese. To make "five-way" chili, start with a layer of cooked beans. For an authentic finish, garnish with crumbled oyster crackers.

Five-Way Cincinnati Chili

2 tablespoons extra virgin olive oil

1 large onion, chopped

2 garlic cloves, minced

3 tablespoons mild chili powder

1 teaspoon ground cinnamon

1 teaspoon paprika

1 teaspoon ground allspice

One 28-ounce can crushed tomatoes

1/2 cup water

2 tablespoons red wine vinegar

2 tablespoons light brown sugar

One 12-ounce package frozen vegetarian burger crumbles

8 ounces spaghetti

1 1/2 cups cooked or canned kidney beans, rinsed and drained if canned

1 cup grated cheddar or soy cheese, for garnish

1 cup chopped red onion, for garnish

1   Heat the oil in a large pot over medium heat. Add the onion and garlic, cover, and cook until softened, about 10 minutes. Add the chili powder, cinnamon, paprika, and allspice, and stir to coat the onion. Add the tomatoes, water, vinegar, and brown sugar, lower the heat, and simmer for 15 minutes. Add the vegetarian burger crumbles, and simmer 20 minutes longer, or until the desired consistency is reached.

2   Meanwhile, cook the spaghetti in a pot of boiling salted water until *al dente*, and drain.

3   Just prior to serving, heat the kidney beans. Spoon a layer of beans in the bottom of each bowl. Top with a layer of spaghetti, then a ladleful of chili, then grated cheese and chopped onion as a garnish.

SERVES 4

Filé powder, which is made from ground sassafras leaves, is an ingredient found in gumbos and other Creole dishes. It is available in most supermarkets and specialty food shops. If you can't find it, leave it out; the chili will still be delicious. Serve this chili over rice, with a bottle of hot sauce out on the table for those who like a little extra kick.

Louisiana Bayou Chili

1 tablespoon extra virgin olive oil

1 cup chopped scallions

2 garlic cloves, minced

3 tablespoons chili powder

1 teaspoon dried thyme

1/2 teaspoon filé powder (optional)

One 28-ounce can diced tomatoes, drained

One 4-ounce can diced mild green chiles, drained

One 12-ounce package frozen vegetarian burger crumbles

1 cup water

1 teaspoon Louisiana hot sauce

1/8 teaspoon cayenne pepper

Salt and freshly ground black pepper to taste

3 cups cooked or canned red beans, rinsed and drained if canned

1   Heat the oil in a large pot over medium heat. Add the scallions and garlic, and cook until the garlic is softened, about 3 minutes. Stir in the chili powder, thyme, and filé powder (if using). Add the tomatoes, chiles, vegetarian burger crumbles, and water. Bring to a boil, lower the heat, and simmer for 10 minutes.

2   Add the hot sauce, cayenne, salt and pepper, and beans, and simmer 20 minutes longer to blend flavors, stirring occasionally. Taste, and adjust the seasonings. Serve hot.

SERVES 4

California olives and avocados combined with the vibrant colors of fresh vegetables contribute to the West Coast mood of this chili. To complete the picture, serve with a bottle of good California wine and some San Francisco sourdough bread.

West Coast Chili

1 tablespoon extra virgin olive oil

1 medium-size onion, chopped

1 red bell pepper, chopped

1 yellow bell pepper, chopped

2 garlic cloves, minced

8 fresh plum tomatoes, diced

1/4 cup tomato paste

3 tablespoons chili powder

1/2 teaspoon dried oregano, preferably Mexican

Salt to taste

1 cup water

1/2 cup dry red wine

3 cups cooked or canned kidney beans, rinsed and drained if canned

2 ripe Hass avocados, diced, for garnish

1/2 cup sliced pitted ripe olives, for garnish

1/2 cup shredded Monterey Jack or soy cheese, for garnish

1   Heat the oil in a large pot over medium heat. Add the onion, red and yellow bell peppers, and garlic. Cover and cook until the vegetables are softened, about 10 minutes. Add the tomatoes, tomato paste, chili powder, oregano, salt, water, wine, and beans. Bring to a boil, lower the heat, and simmer, covered, for 30 minutes, or until flavors are blended and desired consistency is reached, adding additional water if the mixture becomes too dry.

2   Serve the chili garnished with the diced avocado, sliced olives, and shredded cheese.

SERVES 4

Chili was introduced to the rest of the world at the 1904 St. Louis World's Fair. This Midwestern-style chili, with its subtle sweetness and absence of garlic, is delicious even when the world seems unfair.

World's Fair Chili

1 pound poached tempeh (page 8)

1 tablespoon extra virgin olive oil

1 large onion, finely chopped

One 28-ounce can crushed tomatoes

One 4-ounce can diced mild green chiles, drained

3 tablespoons chili powder

1 tablespoon brown sugar

1 tablespoon cider vinegar

1 teaspoon dried oregano, preferably Mexican

1 teaspoon salt

1 cup tomato juice or water

3 cups cooked or canned kidney beans, rinsed and drained if canned

1   Crumble the tempeh and cook it in the oil in a large pot over medium heat until lightly browned. Add the onion, cover, and cook until softened, about 7 minutes. Stir in the tomatoes, chiles, chili powder, brown sugar, vinegar, oregano, and salt. Add the tomato juice and bring to a boil.

2   Lower the heat, add the beans, and simmer for 30 minutes. Serve hot.

SERVES 4 TO 6

Raisins, cinnamon, and slivered almonds give this chili a Middle Eastern, almost Indian, quality. You might try an aromatic rice such as jasmine or basmati to complement the hint of sweetness in the chili.

Sweet and Spicy Chili

1 tablespoon extra virgin olive oil

1 cup chopped onion

2 garlic cloves, minced

4 tablespoons chili powder

2 teaspoons light brown sugar

1 teaspoon ground cumin

1 teaspoon cinnamon

1 teaspoon salt

1/8 teaspoon cayenne pepper

One 28-ounce can diced tomatoes, drained

One 6-ounce can tomato paste

2 cups apple juice

One 4-ounce can diced mild green chiles, drained

1/4 cup seedless raisins

3 cups cooked or canned kidney beans, rinsed and drained if canned

One 12-ounce package frozen vegetarian burger crumbles

4 cups cooked white rice

1/4 cup toasted slivered almonds, for garnish

1   Heat the oil in a large pot over medium heat. Add the onion and garlic, cover, and cook until softened, about 5 minutes. Stir in the chili powder, brown sugar, cumin, cinnamon, salt, and cayenne. Add the tomatoes, tomato paste, apple juice, chiles, raisins, beans, and vegetarian burger crumbles. Bring to a boil, lower the heat, and simmer for 30 minutes. Taste, and adjust the seasonings.

2   Serve the chili over the rice, garnished with the slivered almonds.

SERVES 4

There are nearly as many recipes for firehouse chili as there are firehouses. The versatility and ease of preparation of this spicy one-pot meal makes chili a perennial favorite among firehouse cooks. Serve this one with cornbread, and offer a choice of toppings, such as shredded regular or soy cheese, chopped raw onion, and chopped chiles. For a mild version, use mild chili powder and mild salsa.

Flaming Firehouse Chili

2 tablespoons extra virgin olive oil

1 cup chopped onion

2 garlic cloves, minced

One 12-ounce package frozen vegetarian burger crumbles

One 28-ounce can diced tomatoes, drained

3 tablespoons hot chili powder

1 teaspoon ground cumin

1 teaspoon salt

1 1/2 cups hot salsa, store-bought or homemade (page 81)

1 cup water

3 cups cooked or canned kidney beans, rinsed and drained if canned

1 Heat the oil in a large pot over medium heat. Add the onion and garlic, cover, and cook until softened, about 5 minutes. Add the vegetarian burger crumbles, tomatoes, chili powder, cumin, salt, salsa, and water. Bring to a boil, lower the heat, and simmer for 30 minutes, stirring occasionally.

2 Add the beans, and simmer 15 minutes longer to heat through and blend flavors. Add more water, if necessary, until desired consistency is reached. Serve hot.

SERVES 4

Beer is an ingredient in this hot and hearty chili, but it also makes a great chaser to have on hand to douse the fire of this incendiary dish. The vegetarian burger crumbles are especially flavorful in this recipe. If ground dried chiles are unavailable, substitute a chili powder blend, cutting back on the cumin according to taste.

Beer Chaser Chili

1½ tablespoons extra virgin olive oil

1 large onion, chopped

3 garlic cloves, finely chopped

3 tablespoons ground dried red chiles

1 teaspoon ground cumin

1 teaspoon dried oregano, preferably Mexican

1 teaspoon paprika

1 tablespoon cider vinegar

1½ cups beer

One 4-ounce can diced mild green chiles, drained

3 cups cooked or canned pinto beans, rinsed and drained if canned

One 28-ounce can crushed tomatoes

One 12-ounce package frozen vegetarian burger crumbles

1 teaspoon hot pepper sauce

Salt and freshly ground black pepper to taste

Heat the oil in a large pot over medium heat. Add the onion and garlic, cover, and cook until softened, about 10 minutes. Add the ground chiles, cumin, oregano, and paprika, and stir to coat. Add the vinegar, beer, diced chiles, beans, tomatoes, vegetarian burger crumbles, hot pepper sauce, and salt and pepper. Bring to a boil, lower the heat, and simmer, uncovered, for 45 minutes, stirring often. Serve hot.

SERVES 4

Vegetarian sausage comes in many varieties: frozen pre-cooked "crumbles," lightly seasoned patties, and mild or hot links. The chopped jalapeños make this chili devilishly hot and spicy. A soothing guacamole makes a good accompaniment.

Devil's Food Chili

2 tablespoons extra virgin olive oil

1 large onion, chopped

3 garlic cloves, minced

1 or 2 jalapeño chiles, seeded and chopped

One 28-ounce can diced tomatoes, drained

One 6-ounce can tomato paste

1 cup water

½ cup dry red wine

3 tablespoons hot chili powder

1 teaspoon salt

One 12-ounce package frozen vegetarian sausage links or patties, cooked and crumbled

3 cups cooked or canned black beans, rinsed and drained if canned

1   Heat the oil in a large pot over medium heat. Add the onion, garlic, and jalapeños, cover, and cook until softened, about 10 minutes. Add the tomatoes, tomato paste, water, wine, chili powder, and salt. Bring to a boil, lower the heat, and simmer, covered, for 15 minutes.

2   Add the vegetarian sausage and black beans, and simmer, uncovered, 30 minutes longer, stirring occasionally. Serve hot.

SERVES 4

The abundance of garlic combined with the other spices adds to the rich complexity of flavor in this delicious chili. I like to serve it over pasta or with hot, crusty garlic bread and a salad.

Garlic Lover's Chili

2 tablespoons extra virgin olive oil

1 pound poached tempeh (see page 8), chopped

1 medium-size onion, chopped

8 garlic cloves, minced

3 to 4 tablespoons hot chili powder

One 28-ounce can diced tomatoes, drained

One 6-ounce can tomato paste

2 cups water

One 4-ounce can diced mild green chiles

1 tablespoon light brown sugar

2 teaspoons dried oregano, preferably Mexican

1/2 teaspoon ground cinnamon

1/2 teaspoon red pepper flakes

3/4 teaspoon salt

1/4 teaspoon freshly ground black pepper

3 cups cooked or canned dark red kidney beans, rinsed and drained if canned

1/2 cup sliced pitted black olives

1   Heat 1 tablespoon of the oil in a large skillet over medium heat. Add the tempeh and cook until browned, about 5 minutes. Set aside.

2   Heat the remaining oil in a large pot over medium heat. Add the onion and garlic, cover, and cook until softened, about 10 minutes. Add the chili powder, tomatoes, tomato paste, water, chiles, brown sugar, oregano, cinnamon, red pepper flakes, salt, and pepper. Bring to a boil, lower the heat, and simmer for 10 minutes.

3   Add the beans and the reserved tempeh, and simmer 30 minutes longer. Just prior to serving, add the olives and heat through. Serve hot.

SERVES 4

As relentless in its spicy heat as it is in its flavorful richness, owing to the dry red wine and roasted red peppers, this chili will have you coming back for more. For convenience, use roasted red peppers from a jar. Cornbread is a good accompaniment.

Roasted Red Pepper Chili

1 tablespoon olive oil

1 large onion, chopped

2 garlic cloves, minced

1 or 2 jalapeño chiles, seeded and minced

3 tablespoons hot chili powder

1 cup water

1/2 cup dry red wine

One 28-ounce can crushed tomatoes

Salt and freshly ground black pepper to taste

One 12-ounce package frozen vegetarian burger crumbles

One 9-ounce jar roasted red peppers, coarsely chopped

3 cups cooked or canned pinto beans, rinsed and drained if canned

1   Heat the oil in a large pot over medium heat. Add the onion, garlic, and jalapeños, cover, and cook until softened, about 10 minutes. Stir in the chili powder, water, wine, tomatoes, and salt and pepper. Bring to a boil, lower the heat, and simmer for 20 minutes.

2   Stir in the vegetarian burger crumbles, roasted red peppers, and beans, and simmer 30 minutes longer. Serve hot.

SERVES 4

Texas chili often contains two kinds of meat, one cubed and the other ground. Here cubed seitan and crumbled vegetarian sausage provide the taste and texture variations.

Texas Too-Hot Chili with Cilantro Sour Cream

1 cup regular or soy sour cream

1/4 cup minced fresh cilantro

1/2 teaspoon salt

2 tablespoons extra virgin olive oil

8 ounces seitan, cut into 1/2-inch cubes

1 medium-size onion, minced

1 cup beer

1 cup water

One 6-ounce can tomato paste

3 to 4 tablespoons hot chili powder

1 teaspoon dried oregano, preferably Mexican

1/2 teaspoon ground cumin

Salt and freshly ground black pepper to taste

One 12-ounce package frozen vegetarian sausage links or patties, cooked and crumbled

1 In a small bowl, combine the sour cream, cilantro, and salt and mix well. Set aside in the refrigerator.

2 Heat 1 tablespoon of the oil in a large skillet over medium heat. Add the seitan and cook until browned on all sides, about 10 minutes. Set aside.

3 Heat the remaining oil in a large pot over medium heat. Add the onion, cover, and cook until softened, about 5 minutes. Add the beer, water, tomato paste, chili powder, oregano, cumin, and salt and pepper. Bring to a boil, lower the heat, and simmer, covered, for 30 minutes.

4 Add the reserved seitan and vegetarian sausage, and simmer, uncovered, 10 minutes longer. Ladle the chili into bowls and serve hot, with a dollop of the reserved cilantro sour cream on each.

SERVES 4

The intense flavors of the ancho paste and spicy sausage give this chili a hearty, full-bodied taste. I like to use Morningstar Farms Sausage-Style Recipe Crumbles in this recipe, but any vegetarian sausage will do.

Spicy Vegetarian Sausage and Bean Chili

4 dried ancho chiles, stemmed and seeded

3 garlic cloves

1 tablespoon whole cumin seeds

1/4 teaspoon cayenne pepper

1 medium-size onion, chopped

1 tablespoon extra virgin olive oil

1 teaspoon dried oregano, preferably Mexican

2 cups canned tomato puree

Salt and freshly ground black pepper to taste

One 12-ounce package frozen vegetarian sausage links or patties, cooked and crumbled

3 cups cooked or canned pinto beans, rinsed and drained if canned

1   Plunge the chiles into a pot of boiling water, remove immediately, and drain. Place the chiles in a blender or food processor with the garlic, cumin, and cayenne. Puree and set aside.

2   Heat the oil in a large pot over medium heat. Add the onion, cover, and cook until softened, about 5 minutes. Stir in the reserved chili paste, oregano, tomato puree, and salt and pepper. Bring to a boil, lower the heat, and simmer, covered, for 15 minutes.

3   Add the vegetarian sausage and pinto beans and simmer 30 minutes longer, adding water if the chili is too dry. Serve hot.

SERVES 4

Mix and match beans in this chili according to your preference. This recipe is especially suited to using canned beans for ease of preparation. The smoky taste of the chipotle chile complements the flavor of the beans. Serve with your choice of garnishes, such as shredded cheese, chopped fresh tomato, and minced green bell pepper.

Four-Alarm Three-Bean Chili

1 tablespoon extra virgin olive oil

1 medium-size onion, chopped

3 tablespoons hot chili powder

1 teaspoon salt

One 28-ounce can crushed tomatoes

1 chipotle chile in adobo sauce, minced

1½ cups cooked or canned pinto beans, rinsed and drained if canned

1½ cups cooked or canned dark red kidney beans, rinsed and drained if canned

1½ cups cooked or canned black beans, rinsed and drained if canned

1   Heat the oil in a large pot over medium heat. Add the onion, cover, and cook until softened, about 5 minutes. Stir in the chili powder, salt, tomatoes, and chipotle. Bring to a boil, lower the heat, and simmer for 15 minutes.

2   Add the pinto, kidney, and black beans, and simmer gently, uncovered, 30 minutes longer. Serve hot.

SERVES 4

The sweetness of the corn helps to offset some of the chile heat, but you'll still want to plan a few "cool-down" accompaniments for this fiery chili. True fire-eaters may want to increase the number of chiles, or add a habanero or Scotch bonnet to the pot.

Blazing Three-Chile Chili

1 tablespoon extra virgin olive oil

1 serrano chile, minced

1 jalapeño chile, minced

3 tablespoons hot chili powder

1 teaspoon sugar

1 teaspoon ground cumin

3 cups cooked or canned pinto beans, rinsed and drained if canned

One 28-ounce can crushed tomatoes

2 cups fresh, frozen, or canned corn kernels

One 4-ounce can diced mild green chiles, drained

1 cup water or tomato juice

1 cup grated cheddar or soy cheese, for garnish

Heat the oil in a large pot over medium heat. Add the serrano and jalapeño, cover, and cook until softened, about 5 minutes. Add the chili powder, sugar, cumin, beans, tomatoes, corn, chiles, and water. Bring to a boil, lower the heat, and simmer for 30 to 45 minutes, adding more water if the mixture becomes too thick. Serve topped with the grated cheese.

SERVES 4

This rich, aromatic chili is one of my personal favorites. Fragrant with orange and thyme, it is sophisticated enough to serve at a dinner party. Try it served over basmati rice, accompanied by a crisp white wine.

Orange- and Thyme-Scented Chili

1 tablespoon extra virgin olive oil

1 large onion, chopped

1 red bell pepper, chopped

I jalapeño chile, minced

3 tablespoons chili powder

2 teaspoons minced fresh thyme, or 1 teaspoon dried

1 teaspoon paprika

1 tablespoon light brown sugar

One 14.5-ounce can diced tomatoes, drained

1 cup hot or mild salsa, store-bought or homemade (page 81)

3 cups cooked or canned black beans, rinsed and drained if canned

One 12-ounce package frozen vegetarian sausage links or patties, cooked and crumbled

½ cup fresh orange juice

½ cup water

2 teaspoons fresh orange zest

Regular or soy sour cream, for garnish

Orange slices, for garnish

Thyme sprigs, for garnish

1   Heat the oil in a large pot over medium heat. Add the onion, bell pepper, and jalapeño, cover, and cook until softened, about 10 minutes. Stir in the chili powder, thyme, paprika, and brown sugar. Add the tomatoes, salsa, beans, and vegetarian sausage, lower the heat, and simmer for 20 minutes.

2   Add the orange juice, water, and orange zest, and simmer 15 minutes longer, adding a little water if the chili becomes too dry. Serve the chili garnished with the sour cream, orange slices, and thyme sprigs.

SERVES 6

The addition of strong black coffee adds a hearty richness to this chili. It is said that chuck wagon cooks of the old West often used leftover coffee in their cooking to conserve their supply of fresh water.

Chili Java

1 tablespoon extra virgin olive oil

1 medium-size onion, chopped

2 garlic cloves, minced

3 tablespoons chili powder

1 teaspoon ground cumin

1 cup strong brewed coffee

1 cup water

One 12-ounce package frozen vegetarian burger crumbles

3 cups cooked or canned dark red kidney beans, rinsed and drained if canned

One 4-ounce can diced mild green chiles, drained

1 tablespoon fresh lime juice

1 tablespoon chopped fresh cilantro

Salt and freshly ground black pepper to taste

Regular or soy sour cream, for garnish

1   Heat the oil in a large pot over medium heat. Add the onion and garlic, cover, and cook until softened, about 10 minutes. Stir in the chili powder, cumin, coffee, and water. Bring to a boil, lower the heat, add the vegetarian burger crumbles, beans, and chiles, and simmer for 45 minutes.

2   Stir in the lime juice, cilantro, and salt and pepper, and simmer 5 minutes longer. Serve hot, topping each serving with a dollop of the sour cream.

SERVES 4

Tequila and lime deliver a pungent kick and orange juice adds a subtle sweetness to this party chili. Serve it with your favorite toppings and side dishes, along with a pitcher of tequila sunrises, or maybe some cold beer served in glasses rimmed with lime juice and sea salt.

Tequila Sundown Chili

2 tablespoons extra virgin olive oil

2 cups chopped onion

2 garlic cloves, minced

2 tablespoons chili powder

1 teaspoon ground coriander

One 28-ounce can crushed tomatoes

1/4 cup tequila

2 tablespoons fresh lime juice

1/4 cup fresh orange juice

1 cup water

2 teaspoons dried savory

1 teaspoon salt

1/4 teaspoon freshly ground black pepper

1 tablespoon sugar

3 cups cooked or canned pinto beans, rinsed and drained if canned

1   Heat the oil in a large pot over medium heat. Add the onion, garlic, chili powder, and coriander. Cover, and cook until softened, about 5 minutes. Stir in the tomatoes, tequila, lime juice, orange juice, water, savory, salt, pepper, and sugar. Bring to a boil, lower the heat, and simmer for 15 minutes, stirring occasionally.

2   Add the beans and simmer 30 minutes longer, or until the desired consistency is reached. Serve hot.

SERVES 4

SUPER-SPEEDY

MEALS

Although there are many variations of this traditional dish throughout the Caribbean, it's a special favorite in Jamaica, where the "peas" used are actually red kidney beans. Coconut milk and chile peppers add richness and heat to this tasty and nutritious version, which can be ready in minutes if using cooked rice and canned beans. Accompany with a salad or green vegetable.

Jamaican-Style Rice and "Peas"

1 tablespoon extra virgin olive oil

1 medium-size onion, chopped

2 garlic cloves, chopped

1 to 2 small hot chiles, seeded and chopped

1 teaspoon minced fresh thyme, or ½ teaspoon dried

1 cup unsweetened coconut milk

4 cups cooked long-grain white rice

1½ cups cooked or canned red kidney beans, rinsed and drained if canned

Salt and freshly ground black pepper to taste

Heat the oil in a large skillet over medium heat. Add the onion, garlic, and chiles, cover, and cook for 10 minutes, or until the vegetables soften. Add the thyme and coconut milk, stirring to combine, then stir in the rice and beans and season with salt and pepper. Cook over low heat, stirring gently, until heated through, about 5 minutes. Serve in a shallow bowl.

SERVES 4

This is also known as "Monday night supper" in New Orleans, where virtually every kitchen has a spicy pot of kidney beans simmering on the stove come Monday. Filé powder is made from ground sassafras leaves, and is used to season and thicken gumbos and other Creole dishes. It is available in specialty food shops and in the gourmet section of well-stocked supermarkets. If unavailable, it is okay to omit it.

Louisiana Red Beans and Rice

1 tablespoon extra virgin olive oil

1 medium-size onion, finely chopped

1 small green bell pepper, finely chopped

2 garlic cloves, minced

One 28-ounce can diced tomatoes, drained

3 cups cooked or canned kidney beans, rinsed and drained if canned

1/2 cup water

1/2 teaspoon filé powder (optional)

1 teaspoon Tabasco sauce

1 teaspoon dried thyme, crumbled

1/2 teaspoon salt

1/8 teaspoon cayenne pepper

4 to 5 cups hot cooked long-grain white rice (or try Louisiana pecan rice)

Heat the oil in a large saucepan over medium heat. Add the onion, bell pepper, and garlic, cover, and cook until tender, about 10 minutes. Add the tomatoes, beans, water, filé powder (if using), Tabasco, thyme, salt, and cayenne. Cover and simmer until the flavors have blended, about 10 minutes. Serve over the rice.

SERVES 4

Use either white or brown long-grain rice for this quick and colorful skillet dish made with garden-fresh vegetables. The vegetables can be shredded in a food processor using the shredding disc or with a box grater.

Shredded Veggie Rice

1 tablespoon extra virgin olive oil

1 small onion, shredded

1 large carrot, shredded

1 zucchini, shredded

1 yellow squash, shredded

2 scallions, minced

1 large garlic clove, minced

2 teaspoons grated fresh ginger

3 cups cold cooked long-grain white or brown rice

2 tablespoons tamari

Heat the oil in a large skillet over medium heat. Add the onion, carrot, zucchini, yellow squash, scallions, garlic, and ginger and cook until the vegetables are beginning to soften, about 4 minutes. Add the rice and tamari and cook, stirring and breaking up any clumps of rice, until the rice is heated through, about 10 minutes. Serve hot.

SERVES 4

Black-eyed peas and sweet Vidalia onions from Georgia bring a Southern touch to this all-American fried rice. Vegetarian Worcestershire sauce is available in natural foods stores; use a splash of tamari if unavailable.

Southern Fried Rice

1 tablespoon extra virgin olive oil

1 large Vidalia onion, finely chopped

3 cups cold cooked long-grain white or Texmati rice

One 14.5-ounce can diced tomatoes, drained

2 teaspoons fresh lemon juice

1 teaspoon vegetarian Worcestershire sauce

$1/_2$ teaspoon Tabasco sauce

$1/_2$ teaspoon salt

$1/_8$ teaspoon freshly ground black pepper

$1 1/_2$ cups cooked or canned black-eyed peas, rinsed and drained if canned

$1/_4$ cup minced fresh Italian parsley

Heat the oil in a large skillet over medium heat. Add the onion, cover, and cook until softened, about 5 minutes. Add the rice, tomatoes, lemon juice, vegetarian Worcestershire, Tabasco, salt, and pepper and stir-fry, breaking up any clumps of rice, for about 10 minutes, or until hot. Stir in the black-eyed peas and parsley and cook, stirring, until the peas are hot. Adjust the seasonings if necessary, and serve.

SERVES 4

Short-grain brown rice holds together well and adds a nutty flavor that complements the almonds in these tasty burgers. Serve on their own with a sauce or chutney, or on burger rolls with all the trimmings.

Almond-Rice Burgers

1 cup cooked short-grain brown rice

1½ cups cooked or canned pinto beans, rinsed and drained if canned

1 cup dry bread crumbs

½ cup coarsely ground almonds

¼ cup grated onion

¼ cup grated carrots

½ teaspoon paprika

½ teaspoon salt

⅛ teaspoon cayenne pepper

2 tablespoons extra virgin olive oil

1 In a large bowl, combine the rice, beans, bread crumbs, almonds, onion, carrots, paprika, salt, and cayenne and stir until well blended. Or combine the ingredients in a food processor and process until blended. Shape the mixture into four ½-inch-thick patties.

2 Heat the oil in a large skillet over medium-high heat. Add the patties and cook for about 5 minutes per side, until golden brown. Serve immediately.

SERVES 4

Frozen tofu ravioli are available in natural foods stores, but cheese ravioli, available in most supermarkets, may be substituted. Tender baby spinach is found in most supermarket produce sections, where it is available both bagged and loose for customers to bag as much as they want.

Tofu Ravioli with Baby Spinach and Pine Nuts

1 pound frozen tofu ravioli

2 tablespoons extra virgin olive oil, or more to taste

2 shallots, minced

4 cups fresh baby spinach

Salt and freshly ground black pepper to taste

2 tablespoons pine nuts, toasted

1   Drop the ravioli into a large pot of salted boiling water a few at a time. Cook according to the package directions.

2   While the ravioli are cooking, heat 1 tablespoon of the oil in a large skillet over medium heat. Add the shallots and cook until soft, about 5 minutes. Add the spinach and cook until wilted, about 5 minutes more. Add the remaining oil, season with salt and pepper, and set aside.

3   When the ravioli are cooked, drain and divide them among individual plates. Top with the spinach mixture and pine nuts. Drizzle with a little more olive oil and sprinkle with an extra grinding of black pepper, if desired. Serve immediately.

SERVES 4

Adding toasted hazelnuts to the gremolata gives it a rich flavor and textural interest while elevating the dish to company fare. In addition to serving as an entrée, this dish would make an elegant first course.

Spinach Tortellini with Peas and Hazelnut Gremolata

3 large garlic cloves, finely minced

3/4 cup chopped fresh Italian parsley

1/4 cup chopped hazelnuts, toasted

Zest of 2 lemons

1 pound fresh or frozen spinach tortellini

1/2 cup frozen peas

1/4 cup extra virgin olive oil

Salt and freshly ground black pepper to taste

1 To make the gremolata, combine the garlic, parsley, hazelnuts, and lemon zest in a small bowl and set aside.

2 Cook the tortellini in a large pot of salted boiling water according to the package directions. During the last minute of cooking time, add the peas.

3 When the pasta is cooked, drain the pasta and peas, and place in a large bowl. Add the oil, the gremolata, and salt and pepper, and toss gently to combine. Transfer to individual serving plates and serve immediately.

SERVES 4

Radiatore, or "little radiators," are used in this light and lively pasta dish made with fresh yellow tomatoes. Miso, a concentrated soybean paste, adds a salty richness to this sauce. A traditional Japanese ingredient used to make soups and enrich sauces and dressings, miso is a blend of fermented soybeans and grains that is said to have many health benefits. It is available at natural foods stores.

Lemon Zest and Yellow Tomato Radiatore

1 pound radiatore

1/4 cup extra virgin olive oil

2 large garlic cloves, minced

Juice and zest of 1 lemon

2 teaspoons white miso paste

1/3 cup hot water

3 or 4 yellow tomatoes, chopped (2 to 2 1/2 cups)

2 tablespoons snipped fresh chives

Salt and freshly ground white pepper to taste

1   Cook the radiatore in a large pot of salted boiling water, stirring occasionally, until it is *al dente*.

2   While the pasta is cooking, heat the oil in a large skillet over medium heat. Add the garlic and cook until fragrant, about 1 minute. Reduce the heat to very low, and stir in the lemon juice and zest. Blend the miso into the hot water until smooth and stir it into the sauce. Add the tomatoes and keep warm over low heat.

3   When the pasta is cooked, drain and place it in a serving bowl. Add the sauce, chives, and salt and pepper, and toss gently to combine. Serve immediately.

SERVES 4

Use ridged ziti to help ensure that every bit of the flavorful tapenade will cling to the pasta. For the best flavor, be sure to use good-quality oil-cured olives for the tapenade—canned black olives packed in water simply won't do.

Ziti with Black Olive Tapenade

1/4 cup extra virgin olive oil	2 tablespoons capers
1 small onion, minced	1/2 teaspoon salt
2 garlic cloves, chopped	1/4 teaspoon red pepper flakes, or to taste
1/4 cup oil-cured black olives, pitted	1 pound ziti
1/4 cup chopped fresh Italian parsley	

1   Heat 1 tablespoon of the oil in a small skillet over medium heat. Add the onion and garlic. Cover and cook for 5 minutes or until softened. Transfer the mixture to a food processor and add the olives, parsley, capers, salt, and red pepper flakes. Pulse until the mixture is coarsely blended, about 1 minute. Set aside.

2   Cook the ziti in a large pot of salted boiling water, stirring occasionally, until it is *al dente*. Drain and place in a serving bowl. Add the remaining olive oil and the reserved tapenade and toss well. Serve immediately.

SERVES 4

Meaty chickpeas provide substance to this dish, which is best made in the summer when fresh ripe tomatoes and mint are at their peak. While mint is more commonly thought of as an ingredient in Greek and Middle Eastern cooking, it is favored by Italian cooks as well.

Penne with Tomatoes, Chickpeas, and Mint

1/4 cup extra virgin olive oil

2 shallots, minced

3 or 4 large ripe tomatoes, chopped

1 1/2 cups cooked or canned chickpeas, rinsed and drained if canned

1 bunch scallions, minced

Salt and freshly ground black pepper to taste

1 pound penne

1/4 cup minced fresh mint

1   Heat the oil in a large skillet over medium heat. Add the shallots and cook until softened, about 5 minutes. Add the tomatoes, chickpeas, scallions, and salt and pepper. Simmer until heated through, about 5 minutes. Keep warm over low heat.

2   Cook the penne in a large pot of boiling water, stirring occasionally, until it is *al dente*. Drain and place in a large serving bowl. Add the tomato and chickpea mixture and the mint, and toss gently to combine. Serve immediately.

SERVES 4

Measurement Equivalents

Please note that all conversions are approximate.

LIQUID CONVERSIONS

U.S.	METRIC
1 tsp	5 ml
1 tbs	15 ml
2 tbs	30 ml
3 tbs	45 ml
1/4 cup	60 ml
1/3 cup	75 ml
1/3 cup + 1 tbs	90 ml
1/3 cup + 2 tbs	100 ml
1/2 cup	120 ml
2/3 cup	150 ml
3/4 cup	180 ml
3/4 cup + 2 tbs	200 ml
1 cup	240 ml
1 cup + 2 tbs	275 ml
1 1/4 cups	300 ml
1 1/3 cups	325 ml
1 1/2 cups	350 ml
1 2/3 cups	375 ml
1 3/4 cups	400 ml
1 3/4 cups + 2 tbs	450 ml
2 cups (1 pint)	475 ml
2 1/2 cups	600 ml
3 cups	720 ml
4 cups (1 quart)	945 ml (1,000 ml is 1 liter)

OVEN TEMPERATURE CONVERSIONS

°F	GAS MARK	°C
250	1/2	120
275	1	140
300	2	150
325	3	165
350	4	180
375	5	190
400	6	200
425	7	220
450	8	230
475	9	240
500	10	260
550	Broil	290

WEIGHT CONVERSIONS

U.S./U.K.	METRIC
1/2 oz	14 g
1 oz	28 g
1 1/2 oz	43 g
2 oz	57 g
2 1/2 oz	71 g
3 oz	85 g
3 1/2 oz	100 g
4 oz	113 g
5 oz	142 g
6 oz	170 g
7 oz	200 g
8 oz	227 g
9 oz	255 g
10 oz	284 g
11 oz	312 g
12 oz	340 g
13 oz	368 g
14 oz	400 g
15 oz	425 g
1 lb	454 g

INDEX